RURAL WRONGS

Hunting and the Unintended Consequences of Bad Law

Charlie Pye-Smith

First published
in Great Britain in 2023 by
The R.S. Surtees Society
Marsh Farm
East Woodlands
Frome, BA11 5EL

ISBN 978-0-948560-92-7

THE RS SURTEES SOCIETY

'For every complex problem there is an answer that is clear, simple, and wrong.'

H. L. Mencken, American journalist

*

'Hunting, shooting and fishing create an interest in the species and a desire to conserve their habitats that is matched by virtually no other relation between man and animal – a point that needs no explaining to those who take part in these pursuits, and which can seldom be explained to anyone else.'

Sir Roger Scruton, English philosopher

*

'To me, banning [hunting] was a nonsense issue for a serious party making a determined bid for government after 18 years in opposition. It was best left alone.'

The Rt Hon Jack Straw, former Labour Home Secretary

AN AUTUMN MEET OF THE DUKE OF BUCCLEUCH'S HUNT IN THE SCOTTISH BORDERS.
(CHRIS STRICKLAND)

CONTENTS

Acknowledgements

8

Foreword, by Charles Moore

9

Prologue

10

Chapter 1
TRIBE AND PREJUDICE

13

Chapter 2
EXMOOR: THE LOSS OF RESPECT FOR THE QUARRY SPECIES

21

Chapter 3
THE SCOTTISH BORDERS: TREATING THE FOX AS VERMIN

29

Chapter 4
THE BROWN HARE AND THE UNINTENDED CONSEQUENCES OF BAD LAW

37

Chapter 5
LOWLAND ENGLAND: OPEN SEASON ON THE FOX

47

Chapter 6
THE WELSH EXPERIENCE

59

Chapter 7
ANIMAL RIGHTS, RURAL WRONGS

71

Epilogue

83

Donors, Interviewees and Helpers

88

Index

90

ACKNOWLEDGEMENTS

A great many people provided help and information during the research and writing of *Rural Wrongs*. Some kindly put us up for the night and gave us dinner; all spent hours, occasionally days, discussing the impact of the hunting bans and the state of our wildlife. Most of the people we met feature in the following pages, but a few asked not to be mentioned by name. All made a valuable contribution.

Although I am the sole author of *Rural Wrongs*, this is very much a joint effort between myself and Jim Barrington. Jim's time in the field – amounting to over 50 days – was covered by the Countryside Alliance, for whom he works as an adviser on animal welfare. We would like to acknowledge their generosity and forbearance, as they had no idea what our conclusions would be.

This book would never have been written without the generous support of a significant number of individuals. They not only paid for the time I spent in the field, but for the printing and publication of this book. My thanks go to all of them. They are listed, together with everyone else who helped us, at the end of the book.

It seems invidious to mention here so few among so many, but I would like to thank Charles Moore (Lord Moore of Etchingham) for writing the Foreword. Special mention must also be made of Rob Williams M.F.H. Staff at his company designed the book and organised the printing, and as chairman of the RS Surtees Society he convinced his executive committee that the Society should publish *Rural Wrongs*. I can only hope that the great Victorian author's best known character, Mr John Jorrocks, a vulgar but good-natured sporting cockney grocer, would approve of the contents.

FOREWORD
by Lord Moore of Etchingham

The purported purpose of the Hunting Act, which came into force in 2005, was to improve animal welfare. Those who opposed the ban argued that it would not achieve this. If anything, it would damage welfare. The former quarry species would suffer death by crueller means, and there would no longer be an incentive to keep their populations in balance.

More than enough time has now elapsed to test the proposition of the Act's supporters. This excellent and readable book does so. Using first-hand research from most parts of the kingdom, which he has conducted with the expert and indefatigable Jim Barrington, Charlie Pye-Smith vindicates the Act's opponents. In many places, foxes have been mercilessly shot. Their populations have plummeted. There is associated damage to rural habitats and to the human communities who for so long managed them.

Rural Wrongs is the first serious work of its kind. It contains a wealth of good evidence, but it is not a dry work of reference. It is a vivid and heartfelt tale about what happens to animal and human landscapes when people meddle with them for the wrong reasons. It should serve as a handbook for all those seeking to show why bad law must be replaced by rules that truly address animal welfare.

PROLOGUE

Here are glimpses of the British countryside most people won't see in 2023:

- A dozen foxes hung up on a farm gate in West Wales by the men who shot them the night before – just to show what they've done.
- A pyramid of fox corpses outside the back door of a gamekeeper's house on an intensive shooting estate in Devon.
- Fox cubs starving to death in their earths because their mothers have been killed.
- Broken gates, damaged crops, terrorised farmers and a pile of dead hares on a farm track in East Anglia – the calling card of the illegal hare coursers who plague the eastern lowlands.
- Sick, diseased and injured red deer dying a slow and painful death in forests on Exmoor because huntsmen can no longer use a full pack of hounds to find them.

You can attribute all these things, either entirely or in part, to the 2004 Hunting Act, a piece of legislation that was supposed to make life better for the quarry species, but which in many ways has made it much worse.

In a book published two years after the passage of the 2004 Hunting Act, *Rural Rites – Hunting and the Politics of Prejudice*, I predicted that the legislation would fail to improve wild animal welfare and almost certainly have the opposite effect. That is precisely what has happened.

It may be true that Parliament spent a staggering 700 hours discussing and debating hunting with dogs, but many MPs paid no attention to the facts. They simply wanted to ban an activity carried out by a group of people they despised – snobs and yobs, as one Labour MP memorably called them. They used animal welfare as a Trojan horse, encouraged and guided by animal rights groups.

Astonishingly, neither the organisations which represent hunting, nor the organisations which spent an estimated £30 million on campaigning for a ban, nor the government itself, have commissioned studies to assess the impact of the Hunting Act on the fox, red deer and brown hare. That is the purpose of the Rural Wrongs project, and in the following pages you can read about the ways in which the Act, and its equivalent in Scotland, have affected the welfare of our wildlife. Seldom can a piece of legislation have so dramatically achieved the opposite of its stated intention.

But this is not just a story of political incompetence and unremitting ecological gloom. In the closing pages I suggest how the current legislation could be replaced by a law which will effectively protect wild animals from unnecessary suffering and cruelty, and at the same time – perhaps this is a pious hope – help to create a healthier countryside and a less censorious attitude towards a cultural minority.

Writing about hunting with dogs has provided me, from time to time, with a meagre journalistic income and a great deal of interest. But I have never hunted or followed a hunt for pleasure, nor do I have any intention of doing so. Before the ban came into force in 2005, I tried to make arrangements to interview the then director of the League Against Cruel Sports. "We don't talk to pro-blood sports journalists," I was told by its press officer. I pointed out that I was not so much pro-hunting as anti-bad-law-making. There is an important difference, one which the animal rights lobby is incapable of grasping. It is in that spirit that I have written *Rural Wrongs*.

The evidence provided in the following pages relies on the testimony of a wide variety of people, from ecologists to gamekeepers, landowners to conservationists and hunters. However, there is one significant group whose views are missing: the animal rights and animal welfare organisations which campaigned for the hunting ban. Over many years, the League Against Cruel Sports, the Royal Society for the Prevention of Cruelty to Animals (RSPCA) and the International Fund for Animal Welfare (IFAW) devoted a large amount of time and resources to convincing politicians and the general public that hunting was cruel. They also channelled considerable sums of money into the bank accounts of the Labour Party and its MPs. Since the ban, they have spent not one penny, as far as I know, on investigating its impact on animal welfare. We requested interviews with all three organisations, but were met with uncharacteristic silence. The implication is clear: they know that the ban has failed to do what it was supposed to do, which was improve animal welfare.

HUNTSMAN BARRY TODHUNTER AND FOLLOWERS OF THE BLENCATHRA FOXHOUNDS, ESTABLISHED IN THE LAKE DISTRICT IN 1840.

(CHARLIE PYE-SMITH)

Chapter 1
TRIBE AND PREJUDICE

In its 1997 manifesto the Labour Party pledged greater protection for wildlife. "We have advocated new measures to protect animal welfare, including a free vote in Parliament on whether hunting with hounds should be banned," it said. Seven years later, MPs voted for a ban by a large majority.

I explored how the 2004 Hunting Act came into being in *Rural Rites,* published some 18 months after the Act became law.[1] In the book I made the following claim about the new legislation: "Instead of improving animal welfare – its ostensible aim – it is almost certainly doing the opposite. Furthermore, the Act has alienated a significant chunk of society by proscribing, or attempting to proscribe, an activity enjoyed by tens of thousands of law-abiding citizens."

The Hunting Act, I argued, was so badly drafted that it would be almost impossible to enforce – over 90% of the successful prosecutions under the Act have been for poaching, not for activities carried out by registered hunts – and it was full of bizarre inconsistencies. For example, you can hunt rats and rabbits with as many dogs as you like, but it is illegal to hunt mice or hares with dogs, unless you are pursuing a hare that has been shot or wounded. You can use a terrier to bolt a fox from its earth to protect game birds that you intend to shoot, but not livestock or rare ground-nesting species like curlew or hen harrier. However, you can flush a fox from a woodland with one or two dogs and then shoot it, or try to shoot it. In other words, the Act promotes alternative ways of killing foxes which are more likely to cause suffering than death in the jaws of a pack of hounds.

Many of those who voted for a ban hoped that this legislation would be the end of the matter; that the hunters and their rustic supporters would be consigned to the dustbin of history, to use one of their favourite clichés. Indeed, John Bryant, former director of the League Against Cruel Sports, claimed that within a couple of months of a ban "it would be all over and everyone would wonder what all the fuss was about."[2]

1. *Rural Rites: Hunting and the Politics of Prejudice* by Charlie Pye-Smith, All Party Parliamentary Middle Way Group, 2006.
2. John Bryant of the League Against Cruel Sports, *Daily Telegraph*, 6 January 1996.

How wrong he was. Almost two decades after the Hunting Act became law, the vast majority of registered hunts continue to go out two or three times a week during the hunting season. They may not be pursuing live quarry, except where exemptions under the Act exist or they are deliberately breaking the law, but they still attract large numbers of followers on horseback and on foot, as well as increasingly vicious gangs of hunt saboteurs. Trying to stop the sabs disrupting hunts and beating up the hunters (and sometimes vice-versa) has wasted considerable police time and large amounts of public money.

Rural Wrongs attempts to answer the questions that nobody else has bothered to ask. Has the Hunting Act boosted animal welfare or is it one of those bad laws – to quote Edmund Burke – that represent the worst sort of tyranny? Are the three main species which used to be hunted better off than they were before 2004, or are significant numbers now dying a more horrible death?

CLASS, CASH AND THE TRIBAL GENE

If you want an insight into why the law has failed – hunters and their opponents agree on that, albeit for different reasons – it is important to understand why MPs voted for it in the first place. For a significant number, especially on the Left, it was class and cash, rather than a concern for the welfare of the quarry species, that motivated their support for a ban. Getting the details right was not their chief concern; banning the activities of people they held in contempt was.

"There is not a subject under the sun that is better suited to us [the Labour Party], for raising our morale in the constituencies, than a ban on fox hunting," Dennis Skinner told the House of Commons during a debate in 2004.[3] "This has nothing to do with animal welfare," he said later that year at the Labour Party conference.[4] Hunting, as far as he and many of his colleagues were concerned, was one of the last vestiges of a world in which the inbred, the titled and the landed, lorded it over the common man and woman. Skinner and his fellow travellers saw themselves as the tribunes elected by the plebs to take on the toffs.

There was nothing new in this sentiment. In her portrait of the field sport, *Fox-Hunting*, Jane Ridley recalls how in the 18th century, Whig propagandists caricatured the country gentry as uneducated bumpkins who did little apart from hunt foxes.[5] In Henry Fielding's *Tom Jones*,

3. Dennis Skinner MP, House of Commons, 17 June 2004.
4. Conversation with Jim Barrington at the 2004 Labour Party Conference.
5. *Fox Hunting* by Jane Ridley, Collins, London 1990.

Squire Western was the perfect example: course, unread, untravelled, Tory and frequently drunk. "Country gentleman equals Tory equals fox hunting equals stupid is an association of ideas which still persists," wrote Ridley.

The proof was there for all to see during the hunting debates of the early 2000s. "Hunting was portrayed as people in red coats – toffs, mainly – tearing animals apart for sport," Llin Golding (now Baroness Golding), one of the small number of Labour MPs to vote against the ban, told me when I went to see her. "That's what got most MPs committed to the ban in the first place." This was confirmed by Lord Donoughue, a former Labour minister for farming and the food industry. "I spent 40 years fighting political zealots in the Labour Party and I recognise certain familiar characteristics among those who wish to ban hunting," he said. "They don't care about welfare or cruelty. They just dislike certain people. They are guided by ignorance and prejudice."

Many were happy to air their prejudices in public. "I was proud to vote for the Hunting Act in 2004 to prevent the brutal killing of foxes to satisfy the bloodlust of a few brainless toffs," wrote John Prescott, former Labour deputy prime minister, in the *Daily Mirror* in 2014, ignoring the fact that over 400,000 people, only a small number of whom would self-identify as toffs, joined the Liberty and Livelihood March in defence of hunting in London in 2002. Many other Labour MPs felt, like Prescott, that this was an important battle in the class war.

They had an articulate ally in George Monbiot, one of our more vociferous environmental campaigners and a journalist with the *Guardian*, the great influencer of *bien pensant* opinion. Banning hunting could help to create a classless society, he suggested in an article in September 2004: "As an animal welfare issue, fox hunting comes in at about number 155. It probably ranks below the last of the great working class bloodsports, coarse fishing. It's insignificant besides intensive pig farming, chicken keeping or even the rearing of pheasants for driven shoots. But as a class issue, it ranks behind private schooling at number two. This isn't about animal welfare. It's about human welfare."[6]

It would be absurd to suggest that the vast majority of MPs who voted for the ban were consumed with class hatred. Over a number of years, many had committed themselves to a ban and 75 constituencies had received financial support from organisations like the League Against Cruel Sports. Many had promised their constituency parties – a safe haven for the swivel-eyed in politics – that they would vote for a ban. Besides, the

6. "Class War on the Hoof" by George Monbiot, Guardian, 14 September 2004.

Political Animal Lobby gave the Labour Party £1 million prior to the 1997 general election – an important inducement to deal with the subject once and for all. As the philosopher Roger Scruton observed: "This kind of corruption of the political process elicits no cries of outrage when donor and recipient are both on the left."[7]

There was also a strong tribal element to the vote. Traditionally, the Tories had always been in favour of fox hunting, with odd exceptions like Ann Widdecombe; and Labour had always been against, again with odd exceptions like Kate Hoey (now Baroness Hoey), who came from a farming family in Northern Ireland, and Austin Mitchell, who actually went to the trouble of visiting his local hunt. What became increasingly evident in the years leading up to the ban was that most MPs in the three main parties made little or no effort to explore the subject in detail, for example by reading the report of an inquiry chaired by Lord Burns and commissioned by the home secretary, Jack Straw, who was opposed to the ban.[8] You might quibble with some of the conclusions reached by the Committee of Inquiry into Hunting with Dogs in England and Wales, but it provided a valuable resource about the pros and cons of hunting.[9]

"When Tony Blair eventually writes his memoirs," I wrote in *Rural Rites*, "he will recall his role in the hunting saga with a shudder of regret. Initially, he played to the gallery and lied about his voting behaviour, presumably to garner popularity with the public and his party. In the end, he allowed Tony Banks and his allies to hijack a Government Bill – had he wished, he could simply have dropped it – and he must now live with Lord Jenkins' admonition ringing in his ears. 'Tony,' he told him, 'if you invoke the Parliament Act it will be the most illiberal act of the last century.'"[10] And that's precisely what he did to bypass opposition in the House of Lords.

In his memoirs, *A Journey*, 2010, Blair admitted that the Hunting Act was the domestic legislative measure he most regretted.[11] He had been ignorant about the field sport and was astonished by the amount of trouble caused by the issue, both inside and outside Parliament. "If I'd proposed solving the pension problem by compulsory euthanasia for every fifth pensioner I'd have got less trouble for it," he wrote. When interviewed by Andrew Marr of the BBC, Blair admitted: "I'm not particularly in favour of fox hunting myself, but in the end I came to the conclusion that it was a mistake to have gone down this path."

7. *Green Philosophy: How to think seriously about the planet* by Roger Scruton, Atlantic Books, 2012.
8. See his political memoir, *Last Man Standing* by Jack Straw, Macmillan 2012.
9. *Report of Committee of Inquiry into Hunting with Dogs in England & Wales,* Home Office, 2002.
10. *"True libertarians will support the repeal of the hunting act."* Open Democracy, 16 September 2009.
11. *A Journey* by Tony Blair, Random House, 2010.

By then, of course, it was too late to do anything about it without risking the wrath of his backbenchers. However, he claimed in his memoirs that he managed to get a "masterly British compromise". Hunting, he wrote, "was banned in such a way that, provided certain steps are taken to avoid cruelty when the fox is killed, it isn't banned." I have no idea what this strangulated sentence means; I doubt whether Blair does either. But at least it mirrors the confused nature of the legislation.

A TOUR OF THE NATIONS

Although I am the sole author of *Rural Wrongs* and take full responsibility for everything it contains, this has been a collaborative venture. Over the course of a year, Jim Barrington and I travelled across the country talking to farmers, landowners, gamekeepers, hunters, shooters and others involved in field sports and farming. These are the people at the sharp end of countryside management. We began our journey in the West Country, then made our way to the Scottish Borders, East Anglia, South-east England, Gloucestershire, Lancashire and Wales before visiting Northern Ireland, the last corner of the United Kingdom where hunting with dogs remains legal.

It is worth saying here that the popular image of hunters peddled by people like George Monbiot – "Hunting is a way in which you aspire to become a member of the aristocracy," he wrote in 2004 – is a warped caricature. If this book could talk, you would hear a medley of accents as varied as the landscape through which we travelled. It is true that there is still a smattering of landed gentry on the hunting field, although you are more likely to find them on the grouse moors. A few, to borrow a phrase from Evelyn Waugh, are hopelessly upper class. But most of the hunting people we met on our travels would describe themselves as middle or working class, if indeed they ever thought about their social status: a curious demographic against which to wage a class war.

As I have said, my interest in hunting has been entirely journalistic. Barrington is much more heavily invested in the subject. Hunting, for one reason and then another, has been his life. A former hunt saboteur and executive director of the League Against Cruel Sports, an organisation he left after 15 years of service, he now works as an animal welfare adviser to the pro-field sports opposition, the Countryside Alliance. In the mid-1990s, Barrington came to the conclusion that the leading voices in the League were only interested in a ban on hunting, regardless of how this affected the welfare of the quarry species. After leaving the League, he began to make the case for introducing reforms to hunting that would bring it under proper scrutiny and impose restrictions on certain practices.

At the time, the leaders of the hunting world were convinced they could carry on doing what they had always done and ignore the heckling from the cheap seats. So Barrington's arguments for reform largely fell on deaf ears in the hunting world. He was - and still is - reviled by the anti-hunters, as apostates always are. He did, however, find a new home among a group of MPs who believed that hunting should continue, but with certain restrictions and independent oversight: this was the All-Party Parliamentary Middle Way Group. Led by Labour MP Kate Hoey, Conservative MP Peter Luff and Liberal Democrat MP Lembit Öpik, they commissioned *Rural Rites*.

Rural Wrongs is the sequel. Class warriors like Dennis Skinner may have seen the Hunting Act as a way of destroying the last vestiges of feudalism, but the Act itself is not about creating a more egalitarian society. Poorly drafted though it was, its aim was to improve wild animal welfare. And it is on those terms that we should judge its success or failure.

THE PROSPECT OF A HUNTING BAN ATTRACTED OVER 400,000 PEOPLE TO THE LIBERTY & LIVELIHOOD MARCH IN LONDON IN SEPTEMBER 2002.

(CHARLIE PYE-SMITH)

THE DEVON AND SOMERSET STAGHOUNDS HAVE PLAYED A KEY ROLE IN MAINTAINING A HEALTHY RED DEER POPULATION ON EXMOOR.

(JIM BARRINGTON)

Chapter 2

EXMOOR: THE LOSS OF RESPECT FOR THE QUARRY SPECIES

By the late 1840s, it looked as though the red deer on Exmoor was heading for extinction. After decades of persecution by farmers and poachers there were fewer than 70 left. However, their fortunes swiftly changed once the Devon and Somerset Staghounds enlisted the help and support of tenant farmers. "In a little over a generation or so, the hunt was transformed from being a barely tolerated plaything of a largely absentee gentry, into a thing owned, as it were, by all – at which point opposition to the hunt vanished like summer dew," wrote local historian Jeremy Whitehorn.[12]

Instead of persecuting the deer, which competed for pasture with cattle and sheep, the local community began to protect them. The population rapidly increased – there are now over 3500 red deer on Exmoor – and stag hunting attracted a large following. Over 2000 people turned up for the opening meet in 1876 with picnics for themselves and cash for the hunt. Stag hunting is woven into the cultural fabric of Exmoor's deep wooded valleys, secluded villages and high moors, and most locals still see the deer as a community asset. With stag and hind hunting, the animals are not killed by hounds but dispatched with a special weapon once they are at bay.

The 2004 Hunting Act has had a significant impact on the way deer are managed and perceived. Under the Act, stag hunting has been allowed to continue under the "research and observation" and "rescue" exemptions, but hunts can only use two dogs rather than a full pack. This has made it harder to find and dispatch casualty deer and it has led to deer congregating in greater numbers and becoming more vulnerable to infectious diseases.

Providing a humane end for animals injured in traffic accidents or wounded by rifles and shotguns has always been a significant activity for the three packs of staghounds in the West Country, the Devon and Somerset, the Tiverton and the Quantock. Frequently, the hunts are called out by farmers or members of the public to deal with injured

12. *History of the Devon & Somerset Staghounds* by Jeremy Whitehorn, DSSH Hunt Committee, 2018.

animals under the "rescue" exemption. "When you're only allowed to use two hounds, finding casualty deer becomes much harder than it used to be, when we could use as many hounds as we liked," says Martin Watts, huntsman with the Quantock Staghounds. Before the Act, the hunt used to dispatch 70 or more casualty deer a year; now it is about half that number.

Tom Yandle, former chairman of the Devon and Somerset Staghounds, estimates that his hunt is dispatching about a quarter of the casualty deer that it dispatched before the Act. It is not just that the huntsman and his two hounds are failing to find the casualties they have been told about, it also reflects the fact that a full pack of hounds was far more likely to find casualty deer skulking in the undergrowth on a hunt day. This means that significantly more deer are being left to die a miserable and painful death.

One of the main functions of the hunts has been to break up large herds of deer and disperse them across the countryside. This is important for farmers, as even those most appreciative of the deer want to see the animals moved around so that their neighbours share the inevitable depredations on crops and grassland. Two hounds cannot to do this effectively, and as a result there are much greater densities of deer in certain areas than there used to be.

This has meant two things. Dominant stags are now more likely to cover their daughters than they were in the past, leading to inbreeding; a higher deer density is closely correlated with disease, the most worrying of which is bovine TB, whose management in England costs the taxpayer some £70 million a year and farmers a further £50 million.[13] The disease is causing huge stress and hardship to farmers whose cattle have to be destroyed. The main reservoir for the disease in the wild is the badger, but infected red deer may also have the potential to pass the disease on to cattle.

SPREADING DISEASE

One organisation has been directly responsible for increasing the incidence of bovine TB in the Exmoor deer herd. This is the League Against Cruel Sports, which bought large blocks of land and their sporting rights at Baronsdown and nearby in order to provide the animals with a safe refuge from the hunt. For many years it actively encouraged deer to take up residence by providing supplementary feeding. Herds of more

---

13. DEFRA, *Bovine TB Strategy Review,* October 2018.

than 200 deer often gathered on the small acreage at Baronsdown.[14]

"One year, a load of stillborn deer calves were seen in the woods at Baronsdown," explains Charles Harding, a National Trust stalker, "and we know that red deer in the League's sanctuaries have had serious problems with disease, especially lungworm and bovine TB. That's what happens if you don't manage the herds properly." Of the 97 bovine TB cases confirmed in deer in Devon and Somerset between January 2000 and September 2008, 88 were in red deer and all but 11 were from deer found within 2 km of Baronsdown. An animal rights charity was therefore responsible for not only compromising the welfare of red deer but increasing the prevalence of a disease which could, potentially, have a catastrophic impact on domestic livestock.

Under the Hunting Act's research and observation exemption, the Devon and Somerset Staghounds and the Quantock Staghounds have contributed to a study of bovine TB on Exmoor. Carried out by Dr Keith Collard, former associate professor of biomedical sciences at Plymouth University, the results are revealing.[15] He examined blood samples taken from 54 deer killed by the hunts – the deer are always shot, rather than killed by the hounds – and 52 shot by stalkers. 42.2% of the deer shot on the National Trust's Holnicote Estate tested positive for bovine TB, compared to just 16.6% in areas on Exmoor where the hunt operates.

It is true that a number of the deer selected for culling on the Holnicote Estate looked sick and were identified by the stalker, Charles Harding, as potential TB candidates. Most of these came out as TB-positive. "This would tend to elevate the figure for Holnicote beyond that expected if sampling were random, and it might potentially bias the results," concedes Dr Collard. However, the fact that these sick deer were easily spotted suggests that all is not well on the National Trust estate. "No such sick deer were openly visible on the rest of the moor, and all the deer killed by hunts outside Holnicote were TB free."

The National Trust banned hunting on its estate in 1997. The absence of the hunt, according to Dr Collard, has allowed the deer to congregate in areas where there is a good food supply. His research implies that the lack of disturbance caused by hunting with hounds has led to higher densities of deer and greater levels of TB. Hunting, in short, acts as a prophylactic which helps to maintain a healthy deer population, even if the hunts can only use two dogs.

---

14. ADAS, The Health of the Wild Red Deer of Exmoor, November 2008.
15. *Daily Telegraph 24 January 2023.*

Many local observers say there has been a significant change in attitude towards red deer, largely because hunting is now seen as being less effective than it used to be. "More people are shooting deer – both legally and illegally," says Hugh Thomas, chairman of the Exmoor and District Deer Management Society (EDDMS). "In the past, poachers were ostracised and even farmers shooting deer on their own land – which they had every legal right to do – would find they weren't so welcome in pubs, and sometimes shunned in livestock markets. That's all changing now. As the influence of the hunts is receding, there is less respect for the deer." The increase in poaching has undoubtedly led to more wounding, according to Charles Harding.

The Exmoor herd of red deer is by far the best studied in in the UK. Every year some 400 people – mostly hunt supporters – are involved in a census. Giving evidence before the Hunting Act came into force, the EDDMS predicted that a total ban on deer hunting would lead to a dramatic fall in population as the number shot would steadily rise. Within 10 years, they said, just 10% of the herd would be left. However, hunting has continued, even though in a restricted way, and the deer population actually rose from 2573 in 2004 to 3266 by 2020.

It is widely agreed that there are now too many deer, one of the reasons being that the hunts are killing fewer each year. Before the ban, the Devon and Somerset Staghounds would kill around 140 deer a year, not including dispatched casualty deer. That figure has dropped to around 80, and the hunts kill many fewer hinds – the driver of population growth. Other factors are responsible for the rise in population too. During hard winters, pregnant hinds tend to reabsorb their calves. There have been no hard winters for some 20 years now.

FOXING – THE NEW FIELD SPORT

There is no doubt that the fox has fared much worse than the deer since hunting with a full pack of hounds was banned in 2004. This has less to do with the hunting ban than the dramatic expansion of intensive pheasant and partridge shooting. A generation ago, there were just four or five shoots on Exmoor; now there is at least one big shoot in every valley. A generation ago, they would shoot just one day a week during the season; now many shoot five or six days a week.

Ann Mallalieu, a Labour Party life peer, barrister and current President of the Countryside Alliance, has witnessed the spectacular increase in game shooting on Exmoor over the past half-century. "In the 1960s, there was just one shoot round here," she says when we meet at her home. "Now, there are very few landowners and farmers who don't have a shoot. During the season, the lanes are blocked with Range Rovers, you can't ride a horse in any direction on shooting days and there's a lot more wounding of high birds."

A generation ago, shooting was a good way for people to meet their friends, and they didn't have to be rich to shoot. This has completely changed. "Many of the people who come shooting don't know the other guns," says Baroness Mallalieu, "and they don't even bother speaking to the beaters. Most want to get back to London and tell their friends that they've had a 1000-bird day on Exmoor. Of course, shooting does bring employment and money into an area in much need of both."[16]

This is a high-stakes industry, with guests often paying £16,000 or more a day for 8 guns and routinely giving tips of £100 per gun to head keepers for a good day's shooting. Little wonder then that gamekeepers have become ruthless in pursuit of predators which threaten their birds. Foxing, as it is now called in magazines like *Shooting Times*, has become a field sport in its own right, and ruthlessly effective, thanks to the availability of high-tech thermal imaging and night-vision equipment.[17]

Kelvin Thomas, until recently master of the Tiverton Foxhounds, describes how he dropped in to see a local gamekeeper. "Outside his back door there was a huge pile of dead foxes – maybe 15 or more, including some beautiful dog foxes – and this was his 'crop' from last night. I found it devastating. I thought of everything we had worked for when we were hunting." By this he meant that the hunt had always tried to maintain a balance, taking out the weak and the injured, keeping a healthy population of foxes, and observing a closed season so that the vixens could breed unmolested.

Before the 2004 Hunting Act came into force, hunts had a particularly

---

16. Every year between 40 and 55 million pheasants and red-legged partridges are released on shooting estates. Their biomass probably exceeds the combined biomass of all other British birds. Only about one in three of the released game birds is shot, which means that some 30 million or more are eaten by predators, starve to death, die of disease or are killed in accidents. One estimate suggests that even if just a small proportion of those shot and injured are not picked up, a significant number – over 450,000 – are left to die of their injuries. See, for example, the letter from Martin Whitehead in the *Vet Record*, 7/14 January 2023.

17. It is worth pointing out that many people involved with shooting are unhappy about the current direction of travel. Here, for example, is David Whitby, former head keeper at the Leconfield Estate in Sussex, writing in the *Shooting Times* (May 19, 2022): "Where once the clean kill of a 30- to 40-yard pheasant taken in front was the aim of the Guns, now no shot is deemed too high or too far, regardless of competence. The result of this kudos-seeking practice is the wounding of millions of the very creatures that we should hold in the highest regard…. The large commercial shoots that simply saturate the countryside with pheasants, partridges and ducks must somehow be made to see sense. Bag sizes and many other issues need addressing, whether you argue it is better to shoot more birds less often or fewer birds more often is not the point. Big bags simply do not sit well."

important role during lambing time in the hills. One West Country huntsman told us the story of a farmer on Dartmoor who was losing one of each pair of lambs born. He knew this as all his ewes had been scanned and were expecting twins, yet when he arrived in the fields in the morning he always found singletons. He hired a marksman who shot 17 foxes during the course of a few nights. His lamb losses continued, so in desperation he asked the huntsman for help. The latter swiftly tracked down a mangy dog fox, a vixen and 5 cubs in an earth below a fence post. "I dealt with them," he recalled, "and after that the farmer had no more problems - so the marksman had killed 17 foxes that weren't causing problems."

The sheer scale of killing is astonishing. On some large shooting estates keepers kill 300 or more foxes a year, year after year. Furthermore, there is no closed season and milky vixens are frequently targeted, which means that their cubs will starve to death if no one goes to the trouble of finding their earth. As far as foxes and other predators are concerned, the big shoots, with their vast supply of edible biomass, are like giant take-aways.

"It is strange how people don't seem to mind the intensive killing of foxes, but make a huge fuss about culling badgers with bovine TB," says Tom Yandle, who doesn't allow any fox shooting on the family farm near Dulverton. If there is a problem with a fox killing lambs, he or his son will call a huntsman to pursue it with hounds - a very selective way of finding the guilty party. He recently agreed to let a neighbour release pheasants on his land, provided he didn't shoot any of his foxes. The neighbour shot 15 foxes on his land; none were shot on the Yandles' farm. Shoots on both farms shot the same percentage of pheasants put down, proving, in Yandle's mind, that the eradication of foxes is often pointless, especially when the pheasants have left their pens and are capable of flying. "On the whole, foxes do more good than harm, gobbling up the sick and wounded birds. And what better sight is there on a summer evening than a vixen playing with her cubs outside her earth?"

The staghounds are not directly affected by the intensification of the shooting industry, but it does affect the deer. Many of the valley bottoms are now covered with large pheasant pens and infrastructure such as bridges and tracks. The shoots have also cleared away scrubland and denuded the woodland floor. All the activity during the rearing season - when game birds are classified as livestock, not wild birds - frightens the deer, which move on to higher ground where they concentrate in large, dense herds, possibly leading to the problems mentioned above.

Shooting, when conducted well, is a humane way of killing any animal.

However, unlike hunting with hounds, it is not selective. During the autumn the harbourers, as they are known, identify a particular stag for the hunt to pursue, based on their own knowledge and conversations with farmers and wildlife enthusiasts. This might be a stag with deformed antlers, or one responsible for inbreeding. Later in the season, the hunt focuses on killing the females, the hinds – this being essential to control population growth. With a full pack of hounds, before the restrictions imposed by the Hunting Act, the huntsman could "test" large numbers of hinds and eventually pursue the ones that were left behind – often the weak, the sick and the less agile. This is very much the way that wolf packs operate in the wild, selecting the quarry which is easiest to catch and kill. Two hounds cannot test the hinds in the same way.

Fox hunting, as practiced before the ban, also had a strong element of selectivity. Although hounds would sometimes kill strong and healthy foxes, and deliberately so during the autumn cub-hunting season, they were more likely to catch the halt, the lame and the sick thereafter. Indeed, this was one of the arguments the hunting community always put forward: hunting helped to maintain a healthy fox population. However, it is only partially true. Before the 2004 Hunting Act was passed, some 40% of foxes killed by registered hunts were dug out with terriers and shot. These would often be fit, healthy foxes. Having said that, there is no doubt that the use of hounds to track down individual foxes that are killing lambs is highly selective, unlike the indiscriminate shooting of foxes. More about that in the next chapter on the Scottish Borders.

MASTER AND HUNTSMAN CLAIRE BELLAMY AT THE KENNELS OF THE LAUDERDALE FOXHOUNDS.
RECENT LEGISLATION HAS FORCED THE HUNT TO GIVE UP FOX CONTROL.

(CHARLIE PYE-SMITH)

Chapter 3

THE SCOTTISH BORDERS: TREATING THE FOX AS VERMIN

Since the passage of the Protection of Wild Mammals (Scotland) Act 2002, two factors have conspired to make life more difficult for the fox: the Act itself and the intensification of the game shooting industry. The legislation made it illegal for dogs to chase and kill a fox. Instead, hunts were obliged to use a pack of hounds to flush foxes to guns. Under the old practice, the foxes caught above ground tended to be the injured, sick and unlucky. Under the 2002 Act and its replacement, the Hunting with Dogs (Scotland) Act 2023, which limits hunts to using just two dogs, the young, fit and healthy are just as likely to be killed. Under the old practice, foxes were either killed or they escaped.

At the same time, the pressure on gamekeepers to kill foxes has increased as the rearing and shooting of non-native pheasant and red-legged partridge has become a major land-use, yielding higher profits than traditional farming practices. "Of all the quarry species, the fox used to be the most respected," says broadcaster, former farmer and master of foxhounds, Sir Johnny Scott. "Now, they are just seen as vermin." Here, as in the West Country, foxing has become a favoured field sport for gamekeepers and others, including poachers.

HUNTING WITH A PURPOSE

Hunting with dogs in Scotland is largely carried out by two groups whose aims differ. On the one hand there are the hill packs and fox control clubs, many of which emerged in the 1960s, partly in response to the spread of commercial forestry plantations, which harbour high fox populations. These operate on foot, using dogs to flush foxes from forests or other cover to guns. Their sole purpose is pest control. Records from 15 of 19 Scottish fox control clubs – including three traditional hill packs – show that in 2015 they killed 717 foxes and 685 fox cubs. Their services are paid for by farmers and others who wish to protect livestock and game birds.

Mounted packs, of which there were nine in Scotland when we were doing our research, have a somewhat different purpose. Their aim is to manage the fox population in such a way that it remains healthy and at a level which does not pose too great a threat to farmers' livelihoods. However, there is still an element of pest control, with huntsmen and hounds targeting specific foxes which are causing problems. Some farmers may also insist that when foxes go to ground they must be dug out and shot. The subscribers who ride to hounds, rather than the farmers who benefit from their activities, fund the hunts and their services.

The 2002 Act increased the efficiency of fox control among the mounted packs. "Before the Act, if there were five foxes in a covert, we'd catch the weak and injured foxes," says Tim Allen, amateur huntsman with the Duke of Buccleuch's Hunt. "Now, we will kill all five – including the fit and healthy ones. Hunting is no longer selective." In the Buccleuch country, which covers a large area around Hawick and Kelso, hunting is still the main form of fox control in the high hills and forestry plantations, where shooting is difficult or dangerous. During the spring, Allen frequently responds to "lambing calls" from farmers. Before the 2023 Act came into force he would deal with the offending fox, or foxes, by tracking them on foot with, say, 6½ couple of hounds.

Claire Bellamy, joint master and huntsman of the Lauderdale Foxhounds, a farmers' pack which operates between the Lammermuir Hills and the River Tweed, has a similar story to tell. "The thing that's very difficult for me is that we're shooting fit, healthy foxes – which are the ones that would have got away under the old system of hunting with hounds," she says. She contrasts this with her experience as huntsman with the Spooners and West Dartmoor Foxhounds, in South West England, in the years before the 2004 Hunting Act. "If we killed a fox above ground, it was either because it had made a stupid mistake or there was something wrong with it. Healthy foxes nearly always got away."

According to Bellamy, hunting's selective targeting of foxes which are causing a problem during lambing time helps to protect other foxes. In England and Wales, most sheep farmers now call out marksmen, rather than the hunt, to deal with foxes at lambing time because they feel – rightly, according to many hunters – that using two hounds, rather than say six or seven couple – is inefficient. As a result, the fox population in places like Dartmoor has plummeted. "We never had to worry about the hounds going after a fox when we were trail hunting because they'd all been slaughtered since the Hunting Act came into force," says Bellamy.

A SHOT IN THE DARK

Since she took over as huntsman for the Lauderdale in 2016, Bellamy believes the fox population has declined – not so much because of the hunt's activities, but because of increased pressure from gamekeepers. According to Tim Allen of the Buccleuch, the decline has been precipitous in some areas. "We are killing fewer foxes each year, and seeing many fewer too," he says. "We don't see many litters of cubs now, just the odd ones, and on some estates keepers are very hard on foxes, especially during the breeding season."

As president of the Gamekeepers' Welfare Trust, Sir Johnny Scott has some sympathy for modern gamekeepers, if not the intensive shooting estates which are giving the field sport a bad name. "Long hours and difficult conditions in remote areas are leading to serious mental problems for young keepers," he says. "They're put under huge pressure to kill foxes and other predators to maximise the number of birds that can be shot." The real villains here are not the keepers, but the profit-hungry owners and agents who employ them.

We met Sir Johnny with Ed Swales, a former soldier and security expert who hunts with the College Valley and North Northumberland Hunt, whose country straddles the border between England and Scotland. Swales had recently been in the back of a beaters' lorry on a pheasant shoot and he recalls how the gamekeepers were comparing photos on their mobile phones of their latest fox kills. "It just breaks my heart, but what can you say? They are doing what they're paid to do." One day, when he was out hunting, he came across a pyramid-shaped midden with recently killed foxes piled on top of a decomposing slush of bodies. All around were snares to catch foxes attracted by the stench. They would then be killed and thrown on the midden.

Twenty-five years ago, Swales's hunt could go out three times a fortnight on any of the farms in the Bowmont Valley, on the northern flanks of the Cheviot Hills. Now, shooting has become so intensive that there is only one farm where the hunt can go during the shooting season.

The rural way of life here and elsewhere along the Anglo-Scottish border has been meticulously documented by photographer Chris Strickland. As part of our Rural Wrongs research, he took us on a journey through this area and introduced us to several farmers. Well-run shooting estates, he believes, bring considerable benefits, not just to the local economy but for wildlife too. However, there are a growing number of exceptions, one of the more egregious being a tenanted shoot on a large estate in the Bowmont Valley. "The number of partridge release pens has increased from around 14 to 27 in the last two decades," says Strickland, "and every year 40,000 or more partridge chicks are reared to be shot." Whole hillsides are streaked with bird faeces, making the grass less palatable to hefted sheep. At one time, the company which runs the shoot was using plastic wad cartridges. Instead of being picked up, they were being left to blow into the Bowmont River. "That's a lot of plastic," says Strickland.

Then there is the war on foxes. "I don't mind grouse moor keepers being ruthless with foxes – the grouse are wild birds, and alongside ground-nesting birds such as curlew, they are extremely vulnerable, so the keepers have got a reason to be ruthless," says Strickland. The intensive partridge shoots in the Borders are a different matter. "They put down huge numbers of birds and hammer the foxes. Yes, foxes will take a few dozen partridge, but they don't need to kill them all."

THE FARMERS' PERSPECTIVE

One of the farmers we meet – he asks not to be named – has 450 acres of grazing land in the Borders. He and his wife follow the local hunts when they meet on or near their farm on a quad bike. There are now many fewer foxes than they used to be. "In the old days, the hunt might get nine foxes in a day; now they're lucky to get one or two," he says. High-powered rifles with thermal and night-vision equipment have dramatically increased the efficiency of shooting. He knows one keeper who has 142 GPS sites on his mobile phone identifying exactly where every fox hole is. So that makes it much easier for the terrierman to deal with them."

Does he not welcome this, being a sheep farmer? "I don't want to see any foxes at lambing time, but that doesn't mean I want them to disappear," he replies. "Once our lambs are 6 to 8 weeks old, if I see a litter of fox cubs, I will leave them. If you want to get rid of foxes, then get marksmen in. If you just want to control their numbers and have some sport, get the hunt in."

Higher up the valley, we meet another farmer whose land commands fine views across the Cheviots. "In the 1970s, when none of these hills were keepered, the area was heaving with foxes," he says. A group of local farmers set up a fox cub and paid its members to kill foxes. In those days, they were poisoned, shot and snared and fox skins fetched a good price. The fox club later disbanded but there is still a large population of foxes up here – too large as far as many farmers are concerned.

"The partridge shoots are like a vast McDonald's for foxes and other vermin," he says, "and then we get all the foxes coming out of the Otterburn Ranges on the other side of the border." As this is a military area, rifles can't be used to kill foxes and the hunt can only go there with two hounds rather than a full pack, thanks to restrictions under the 2004 Hunting Act. This means that foxes are thriving, as they are in the Sitka spruce plantations which have expanded rapidly in the Borders.

In the early months of the year, he hires a marksman who comes for three or four nights. He will kill around 30 foxes. And the Border Hunt will kill two or three foxes when it comes. "The truth is that there are far too many predators, largely because of the shoots and the forestry," he says. Over the last few decades, the population of ground-nesting birds – curlew, lapwing, redshank – has been decimated by badgers, foxes, ravens and carrion crows. They also pose a significant threat to livestock.

POOR LAW

In 2015, Lord Bonomy, a distinguished judge, was invited by the Scottish Government to undertake a review of the Protection of Wild Mammals (Scotland) Act 2002 to ascertain whether it was providing a sufficient level of protection for wild mammals while allowing effective and humane control where necessary. Drawing on research by the Macaulay Land Use Research Institute (MLURI), Lord Bonomy noted that prior to the 2002 Act mounted hunts accounted for about 540 foxes each year and hill packs some 850.[18] Lord Bonomy speculated that at the time he was carrying out his investigation the mounted packs might be killing more foxes as they were using firearms, but there was no reason to think the number killed each year exceeded 800. He cites the seasonal summary for 2015/16 produced by one mounted hunt. One hundred foxes were roused and 94 shots fired: 54% were killed by the guns, 19% by the hounds and 27% were dug out using terriers.

There are two things to note here. First, approximately one-fifth of the foxes killed by this pack were killed by hounds. According to everybody we spoke to, this inevitably happens when hounds are used to flush foxes: they will sometimes catch and kill the weak and the injured before they get to the guns. So the law, as it stood, was not fit for purpose. Furthermore, even skilled shooters will sometimes wound rather than kill. In most cases, the hounds will be able to track the foxes down. However, injured foxes sometimes get away, possibly to die a slow and painful death.

Secondly, it is worth noting the significance of digging out. "Many farmers will say to us: if you're coming on my land, you need to bring the terrierman," says Tim Allen of the Buccleuch Hunt. In an average

---

18. *Report of the Review of the Protection of Wild Mammals (Scotland) Act 2002.*
    sct0917041518-1_wildmammals.pdf (consult.gov.scot).

year, he reckons that 40% of foxes killed by the Buccleuch are dug out and shot, having been located or flushed from their underground lairs by terriers – "especially in the hills, which are riddled with holes."

Lord Bonomy suggested the government should consider restricting the number of terriers that can be used for digging out to just one dog. However, evidence provided in June 2022 by the National Working Terrier Federation (NWTF) to the Rural Affairs, Islands and Natural Environment (RAINE) Committee suggested that in some circumstances one terrier would fail to flush out a fox, for example under a rocky scree or windblown plantation, whereas two would succeed.

More significantly, Bonomy recommended that hunts should still be allowed to use a full pack of hounds, rather than just two dogs, as is the case under exemptions in the hunting legislation in England and Wales.

A peer-reviewed scientific paper published in the Wildlife Society Bulletin in 2018 describes how the authors, Jeremy Naylor and John Knott, used a pack of hounds and a pair of hounds to flush foxes to waiting guns from some 80 coverts in Scotland.[19] When using a pair of dogs, 56% fewer foxes were flushed. When using a pack, the time to the first fox being flushed was 2.94 times less than with two dogs, and the time from the start of active pursuit of the first fox flushed was 5.05 times less. In other words, using a pack of hounds is far more effective than using just two dogs.

"Conclusions have to be based on evidence," wrote Lord Bonomy in his report. Yet the Scottish government ignored his recommendation and passed a new law in 2023 which restricts hunts to using two dogs.[20] Experience in England and Wales proves that this will be far less effective than using a full pack, and totally ineffective in large areas of forestry. It will also have a prejudicial effect on animal welfare. "If you put just two dogs into a large block of forestry, they could spend all day running after the same fox – that's not good for either the dogs or the fox," says Claire Bellamy of the Lauderdale. Because of the new highly restrictive law, the Lauderdale decided to switch from hunting with hounds to pursuing humans with bloodhounds.

To conclude, the evidence we gathered suggests the 2002 Act has made

---

19. Naylor, Jeremy RJ, and John G. Knott. "A pack of dogs is more effective at flushing red foxes to guns than a pair." *Wildlife Society Bulletin* 42.2 (2018): 338-346.
20. If farmers and landowners wish to use more than two dogs they must apply for a licence, but as the SNP's environment minister said on the day the Hunting with Dogs Bill was passed, the licence would be "an exception to an exception, it will be construed very narrowly and it will only be available where there is no other effective method." Scotland approves tougher crackdown on hunting with dogs (telegraph.co.uk).

the killing of foxes more efficient and less selective. This does not mean that it has made it more humane. Under traditional hunting practices, foxes were either caught or killed. Now they can be wounded. The 2023 Act restricts hunts to the use of two dogs and this will make hunting so ineffective that many landowners will call on marksmen and terriermen to control foxes, rather than invite hunts onto their land. From the point of view of animal welfare and conservation, this could make life worse for the fox, not better.

ARRON ATMORE WAS THE LAST SLIPPER AT THE WATERLOO CUP, THE PREMIER EVENT IN THE HARE COURSING CALENDAR BEFORE THE FIELD SPORT WAS BANNED IN 2005.

Chapter 4

THE BROWN HARE AND THE UNINTENDED CONSEQUENCES OF BAD LAW

The 2004 Hunting Act came into force on 18 February the following year. "Over the next three days, 3000 hares were shot on two estates in East Anglia," says Sir Mark Prescott, racehorse trainer and a leading figure behind the Waterloo Cup, hare coursing's premier event. "That tells you all you need to know about the impact of the Hunting Act." It would have taken legal coursing, under National Coursing Club rules, almost 20 years to kill as many hares if it had been allowed to continue. In its final year, fewer than 170 hares were killed in official coursing events, a tiny fraction of the number of hares shot each year.

The hares on these two estates weren't shot to provide game for the table, although they did that too, but to deter gangs of illegal poachers from invading the land. If ever there was an example of the unintended consequences of bad law, this was it. The Hunting Act, which made it an offence not only to course a hare, but participate in a coursing event or allow coursing on your land, transformed the brown hare – possibly introduced to Britain by the Romans for coursing and hare hunting – from a respected quarry species to vermin in some farmers' eyes. It also led to a dramatic increase in rural crime and violence. Illegal coursing, which before the Act meant setting dogs on hares without a landowner's permission, often on Sundays, had been a problem for decades. However, within a few years of the ban, this sort of poaching had become a much more serious issue, with gangs threatening, and frequently attacking, anyone who tried to stop them coursing, smashing gates, driving across crops and spreading fear. Illegal coursing has become big business, with the value of dogs – the best hare-killing lurchers can fetch over £20,000 on the dark web – reflecting the large sums of money spent on betting, with some events being live streamed so people elsewhere, allegedly as far away as China, can place bets.

SPLITTING HARES

There are two quite different field sports involving the hare: hare hunting using scent hounds like beagles, harriers and basset hounds, and hare coursing, which in a formal sense involves testing the skills and stamina of two greyhounds as they chase a hare. Both are of great antiquity. The Greek philosopher Xenophon's *On Hunting*, written in the fourth century BC, provides a comprehensive description of hare ecology and hunting.[21] Arrian the Greek's *On Coursing*, written around 180 AD, does much the same for coursing, whose history stretches back to Ancient Egypt.[22]

Before the hunting ban it was estimated that hunting with scent hounds, mostly conducted on foot, accounted for around 1500 hares a year. To put this in context, it wasn't uncommon for hare shoots to kill 800 hares in a day. Anti-hunting campaigner Professor Stephen Harris, whose close association with the League Against Cruel Sports raises questions about his impartiality, conceded that "hunting with hounds poses no discernible threat to the hare population."

In 1998, Jim Barrington and I spent some 20 hours following six different packs of hare hounds. Between them they killed just one hare. One of the hunts killed three hares in 30 outings that year; another just one in 42 outings. Matthew Higgs, chairman of the Association of Masters of Harriers and Beagles (AMHB), estimates that before the ban his hunt killed one hare for every three outings, or about 20 hares a year. Some packs would catch more; many would catch fewer.

As a method of controlling numbers, hare hunting was an irrelevance, except in some specific circumstances, for example when undertaken to protect young woodlands and in areas where row vegetables were grown. It is also worth pointing out that hare hunters monitored populations in the areas where they hunted; they were often the only ones to do so across farm boundaries and on a large scale. Members of the AMHB continue to record the number of hares they see when out hunting – some packs pursue rabbits now rather than an artificial trail – although not as effectively as they did before the ban.

Hare coursing has always stirred greater opposition than hare hunting, inspiring numerous private members bills to ban it from the 1930s onwards. With its large working-class following – 80,000 people attended the Waterloo Cup in 1876 – hare coursing was a "barbarous anachronism" as far as Harold Wilson, twice prime minister between 1964 and 1976, was concerned. During the Portcullis House hearings on

---

21. *Xenophon on Hunting: 13 (Studies in Classics S.)* 2001. Editor: Ralph E. Doty.
22. Arrian on Coursing: *The Cynegeticus of the Younger Xenophon,* Translated from the Greek, J Bohn, 1831.

hunting with dogs in 2002, Alun Michael, Labour's rural affairs minister, refused to even take evidence on hare coursing or stag hunting, both of which, in his opinion, were indefensible.[23]

The rules of competitive hare coursing were laid down during the reign of Elizabeth I. They stipulate that two dogs chase a single hare in open country; "a sort of libertarian dog racing without the bother of a track," as the American satirist PJ O'Rouke put it. The dogs, nearly always greyhounds, are given a score based on their ability to overtake and turn a hare. Killing is not the purpose of the sport. "If the hare is fit and healthy it lives. If it is old, stupid or clumsy it dies – this is called natural selection," says Sir Mark Prescott. "Hare coursing was a field sport that encouraged enormous numbers, and the fewer killed the better the day's sport."

CONSERVING THE HARE

Before the ban, hares benefited from conservation measures on coursing estates in England. "The nature of the sport meant that large numbers were required," says Arron Atmore, Pennine farmer, architect and the last slipper at the Waterloo Cup. His job as slipper was to unleash two competing greyhounds, giving the hare at least an 80-yard start. "I would choose hares with the greatest chance of escaping the dogs, and for every hare I chose there would be four or five which I let pass," he recalls. That meant that for a three-day event like the Waterloo Cup, first held at Altcar in Lancashire in 1836, the 150 or so courses required about 1000 hares.

Drawing on the detailed records kept by the National Coursing Club for the last two full coursing seasons in 2003 and 2004, Atmore has calculated that the 24 coursing clubs in England met around six days each season – which adds up to 144 days of coursing. At each meeting there would be some 50 courses, or just over 7000 courses all told. "For every hare you coursed, you ignored around five hares," says Atmore. That implies there would have been around 36,000 hares present on the land which was coursed. Bearing in mind that the beaters driving the hares towards the slipper only covered about 20% of each estate, the population of hares on coursing estates could have been as high as 180,000, which is approximately a fifth of the current UK hare population, according to estimates by the Game and Wildlife Conservation Trust (GWCT).

23. Prior to the Hunting Act there was another group of individuals who hunted brown hare, as well as rabbits and other quarry, using lurchers and long dogs. Frequently, they would go out alone or in small groups and ask for landowners' permission to hunt on their land. Although the number of lurcher hunters has undoubtedly decreased since the 2004 Act, they can still hunt rabbits, providing they get permission from landowners to do so.

As five hares can eat as much grass as one sheep, farmers need some encouragement to tolerate high numbers. At Altcar and elsewhere, they were frequently paid by coursing clubs for crop damage caused by hares. "We used to work very closely with farmers and estate owners," says Atmore. "We encouraged them to leave broad headlands and plant cover crops to provide shelter from predators. We built bridges over dykes so hares could escape dogs or foxes. At weekends we would often organise patrols to stop poachers invading the land." All this came to an end with the 2004 Hunting Act.

A fine example of how much care was put into conserving hares on coursing estates comes from Norfolk. The owner of Little Massingham, Mary Birkbeck, trained the 1973 winner of the Waterloo Cup, Modest Newdown, and her traditional shooting estate hosted some six or seven meetings of the Kimberley and Wymondham Coursing Club every year, as well as regular whippet coursing events. "When I arrived at Little Massingham," recalls Duane Downing, her gamekeeper during the years before the hunting ban, "the first thing she did was present me with a list of priorities – and at the very top was the brown hare, above the wild pheasant and partridge and the farming interests. She was absolutely passionate about hares and it influenced everything we did on the estate."

At the heart of the estate were two fields covering some 30 acres which were known as "the running ground". These were sown with a grass-clover mix and completely de-stoned to benefit the hares. "If I found a dead hare, Mary Birkbeck would tell me to go to the vets in Norwich to get an autopsy – no expenses spared," says Downing. "She wanted to know whether something we'd done on the farm was responsible." After one incident, a hare was found to have been poisoned by a herbicide sprayed on winter stubble. She immediately stopped the practice. When Mrs Birkbeck discovered that hares and other wildlife were ingesting an aldicarb insecticide sown with sugar beet she got together with neighbouring landowners to campaign for a change in its formulation. The chemical company agreed. "If you look after the hare and partridge, it's good for all the wildlife," says Downing.

Downing often used to see 60 or 70 hares in a single field at Little Massingham. He left soon after the ban but Arron Atmore has been back more recently. He often acted as the slipper here during coursing meetings. "In the past, you'd easily put up 30 or 40 hares when you were wandering around. I went back recently and I just thought: where are they?" They have largely disappeared – and this is precisely what Duane Downing said would happen when he made representations on behalf of coursing to one of the final committee meetings on hunting in the House of Lords in 2004.

You could tell a similar story for many other coursing estates. For example, the number of hares on Altcar is probably a quarter of what it used to be, partly because gamekeepers have reduced the population to keep the poachers away, partly because of illegal hare coursing – although the police have much reduced this in recent years – and partly because hares are no longer imported to supply the raw material for the Waterloo Cup from other parts of the country.

Hare coursing and hare hunting were banned in Northern Ireland under the Wildlife and Natural Environment Act (Northern Ireland) 2011. Before the ban, the devolved government commissioned numerous studies on the hare population, but since then virtually no new research has been carried out, so it is hard to tell what has happened to the hare. In contrast, we have a much better understanding about its status in the Republic of Ireland, where park coursing, which involves muzzled greyhounds pursuing a hare on an enclosed strip of grass, remains a popular sport.

In the Republic, each coursing club has a number of discrete localities known as "preserves", managed in a such a way as to encourage high hare numbers. The clubs ban hare shooting on the preserves, practice predator control – according to research by GWCT, one fox family is capable of eating all the leverets produced by the local hare population – and enhance the habitat to encourage hares. In peer-reviewed research published in 2010, scientists from Queen's University, Belfast, revealed that hare density was up to 18 times higher on hare preserves than in the rest of the countryside.[24] There are three possible reasons for this: clubs were either selecting areas with high hare density; they were actively managing preserves to increase abundance; or a mix of the two. It is almost certainly the latter.

Hares are so numerous in some parts of England that they are an agricultural pest and shot in large numbers. These are also the areas where there is the greatest threat, to both farmers and hares, from illegal coursing, or poaching. Despite this, some farmers still go out of their way to conserve the hare. Shortly before we met Robert Bucknell on his arable farm in Essex, he used his thermal imaging equipment, normally reserved for shooting foxes at night, to count 153 hares on three fields covering 84 acres.

---

24. Reid, Neil, Ciarán Magee, and W. Ian Montgomery. "Integrating field sports, hare population management and conservation." *Acta Theriologica* 55.1 (2010): 61-71.

"When I was young, the gypsies round here always had a couple of running dogs under their caravans which they used to catch hares for the pot," he recalls. "If we had a problem with hares on the sugar beet, we'd get the gypsies to sort them out." Before the hunting ban, he and many other farmers would allow a family of gypsies or travellers – the terms encompass a range of groups with different histories, cultures and beliefs – to course hares on their farms. This was perfectly legal. "The deal was they'd keep other people off my land."

This social contract came to an end with the Hunting Act and within a few years illegal coursing became a much more violent affair, frequently attracting people involved with organised crime. With illegal coursing, it is the killing of hares that counts as far as spectators and those placing bets are concerned, not the skill of the chase associated with the sport under National Coursing Club rules. Some of Robert Bucknell's farming neighbours shoot every hare they see on their land to keep the poachers away. He doesn't, but he has paid a price in terms of intimidation and violence. "I've had steel balls fired at me from catapults, knives drawn on me and my vehicle smashed up," he says.

Richard Negus, field sports journalist and professional hedge-layer, has also observed how the type of people involved in coursing has changed on the shooting estates around his home in Suffolk. "Before the ban, the coursers were mostly the sort of people who read *Earth Dog, Running Dog*," he says. "They'd asked for the farmer's permission and from the farmer's point of view it made sense to have some trusted individuals on their land who would beat the bejesus out of anyone else who came uninvited." Nowadays, the poachers are much more likely to be people from outside the community, or people associated with other rural crimes such as farm vehicle theft. "I think the poaching we see now is a direct consequence of the 2004 Hunting Act."

THE IMPORTANCE OF GAMEKEEPERS

"Hares are thriving right now round here, thanks to changes in farming practice and the way that shooting goes hand-in-hand with conservation," says Negus. Many of the shoots in this part of Suffolk rely on wild birds, rather than reared poults, and they have signed up to environmental stewardship schemes which involve, among other things, looking after field margins and planting cover crops. This is not only good for ground-nesting species, but for the hares as well. Predator control, and especially the shooting of foxes, also benefits hares.

When Geoff Garrod arrived at Audley End Estate in Essex as a young keeper in 1984, he could count the number of hares on the fingers of one hand. Now, there is a large and thriving population and on some days you will see 40 or 50 in just one field. He attributes this to predator control – he and his colleagues shoot some 200 foxes a year, including urban foxes which have been dumped by pest control operators from towns – and habitat management. The estate plants significant acreages of bird cover each year and the vegetation within 6 metres of all watercourses is protected. "We look after our birds of prey as well," says Garrod. "We've got eight species and our conservation work fits very happily with what we do for shooting."

But it comes with a cost: illegal coursing. "In the late 1980s, we'd get illegal coursers every day of the week, but over the years more police resources were put into tackling the problem and by the time the hunting ban came in it was pretty much under control," he recalls. For four or five years after the ban, there was little illegal coursing, then it suddenly took off again as the police had let their guard down. "It was much more sinister this time and we became a target for the poachers. There is a huge amount of money involved. One chap I stopped told me he'd just lost 10 grand on a bet. They come in souped-up 4x4s and they easily lose us and the police if we chase them across the fields."[25]

Instead of shooting the hares and depriving the poachers of their quarry, as some farms do, the estate where Garrod works has invested heavily in protective measures. "We've spent over £40,000 in the last three years, installing iron gates with heavy padlocks, and digging deep 2m-wide trenches around the fields so they can't get on with their vehicles," says Garrod. "And I'm glad we do. I love seeing hares running around the fields."

At 11am one Sunday, two men in balaclavas used their vehicle to ram the kennels where Garrod keeps his dogs. Fortunately, his wife disturbed them and they made their getaway without managing to steal the spaniels and terriers. "Trying to steal Geoff's dogs – that really triggered it for me," says Ed Coles, gamekeeper on a 2000-acre shooting estate in Cambridgeshire. "I know they were working dogs, but it's like stealing someone's children. And that's when I set up the petition."

The petition, which swiftly gained some 14,000 signatures, called for much stricter penalties for illegal hare coursing and led to changes in the law. Amendments to the Police, Crime, Sentencing and Courts Bill introduced two new offences: trespassing with the intention of using a dog to pursue a hare; and being equipped to trespass for that purpose. The

---

25. One of the farmers we interviewed said that illegal coursers often leave a pile of 10 to 15 hares in a prominent place as a calling card, as if to say: "We've been here and you didn't catch us."

law, which came into force on August 1, 2022, now allows the courts to impose unlimited fines and up to 6 months in prison. Just as importantly, the courts have the power to make anyone convicted of an offence pay the kennelling costs for their dogs – this could be up to £10,000 – and disqualify them from owning a dog.

"The certainty of the loss of their dogs is their biggest fear," says Robert Bucknell. "Going equipped to commit a crime is the most useful law in stopping them, and then taking all their dogs, phones, knives, catapults, vehicles and even cash from illegal betting. No dogs, no coursing!"

During the last year or so, the extent of illegal coursing has diminished, according to Coles. This is largely because the police have made a greater effort to clamp down on the activity. Operation Galileo, a national policing initiative jointly led by the Lincolnshire police and the National Wildlife Crime Unit, has had a significant impact.

A borderless response to tackling illegal coursing established by police forces in Kent, Bedfordshire, Cambridgeshire, Hertfordshire, Norfolk, Suffolk and Essex has also made a difference. Needless to say, the costs to the taxpayer of clamping down on illegal coursing have been considerable.

"I'm very pleased about the changes in the law and the harsher penalties," says Coles, "but you've still got to catch the illegal coursers." In the past, key witnesses have been unwilling to appear in court for fear of retribution, and this could remain a problem. In the meantime, many estate owners continue to shoot all the hares on their property. This is one of the legacies of the 2004 Hunting Act. Instead of improving the welfare of the hare, it has been more a case of: Cry "Havoc!" and let slip the dogs of war.

According to Sir Mark Prescott, the longest period of time it took from a hare being caught by a greyhound at the Waterloo Cup to it being killed, either by the dog or a steward, was 1 minute 12 seconds. "It seems like a lifetime when you hear a hare screaming, but I know that when I die, if I only suffer for 1 minute 12 seconds, I'll settle for that," he says.

He lists all the things that coursing clubs and gamekeepers did for hares on coursing estates: they encouraged farmers to plant cover crops and look after field margins, constructed bridges over streams and ditches, controlled predators, chased away poachers, and compensated farmers for hare damage. "And all the hares had to do was run like hell one day a year! I think that was a pretty good deal." Especially when you remember that 70–80% of leverets die in the first month of life, and that shooting hares often leads to wounding and a painful, drawn-out death.

RIDERS AND HOUNDS WITH THE SPOONERS AND WEST DARTMOOR HUNT.

(JIM BARRINGTON)

Chapter 5

LOWLAND ENGLAND: OPEN SEASON ON THE FOX

Whether there are too few foxes, just the right number or too many depends on your perspective. Animal rights activists deplore all forms of culling, so presumably there can't be too many for them. In contrast, most commercial shooting operations see foxes as vermin, to be eradicated whenever possible. For sheep farmers and conservationists trying to protect lambs and ground-nesting birds, the fewer foxes on their land during the breeding season the better. Having said that, many conservation organisations are so squeamish about predator control that they now preside over declining populations of the vulnerable species they claim to be protecting.

There is much uncertainty about the number of foxes in the UK. The pre-breeding fox population was put at 240,000 by a study published in 1996.[26] An analysis by the Department for Environment, Food & Rural Affairs (DEFRA), published in 2015, came up with a higher figure of 430,515 foxes.[27] Three years later, a report by Natural England and the Mammal Society suggested that the pre-breeding fox population was 357,000.[28] Dig deep into the various methods used to measure fox abundance and you soon realise that these figures are little more than educated guesses. "There is no single reliable source of data on the fox population," says Mike Short, predation ecologist at the Game and Wildlife Conservation Trust (GWCT) and an expert on fox population dynamics.

What we do know is that the average vixen produces five cubs a year, which means that a population of 240,000 foxes in the spring would rise to around 665,000 by the autumn. Assuming the population is roughly the same the following year, over 400,000 foxes die before the next breeding season. Hunting with dogs probably accounted for around 20,000 foxes a year before the ban – or one out of every 20 foxes that died between autumn and spring. Shooting, snaring, digging out, road

26. Fox - Game and Wildlife Conservation Trust (gwct.org.uk).
27. DEFRA red fox research_1.pdf (mammal.org.uk).
28. Mathews F et al, *A Review of the Population and Conservation Status of British Mammals: Technical Summary*. Natural England, 2018.

accidents, old age and disease accounted for the rest.

Two annual surveys provide an insight into the state of the fox population in the UK. These are the GWCT's National Gamebag Census (NGC), which has been collating shooting records from some 700 estates in the UK since 1961, and the British Trust for Ornithology's Breeding Bird Survey (BBS), established in 1996. The latter encourages ornithologists to record the presence of nine mammals, one being the fox. Both surveys use an index which acts as a proxy for abundance over time, based on foxes killed for the NGC and foxes seen or detected for the BBS.

The NGC records suggest that the UK fox population tripled between 1961 and the early 2009, since when there has been just a slight rise.[29] In contrast, the BBS registered a 41% decline in its index between 1996 and 2016, with the fall being especially steep after 2008.[30] This figure has been seized on by people in the hunting world as definitive evidence that the 2004 Hunting Act has led to a rise in persecution and a decline in numbers.

There are two problems with this thesis. First, cause and effect: if there has been a decline, then other factors – such as an increase in the intensity of shooting to protect game birds – could be more significant than the hunting ban. Second, population estimates based on daytime sightings of a species which tends to be shy and largely nocturnal could be unreliable. "If you're doing a bird survey properly, you don't have the time, and may lack the skills, to accurately identify evidence of fox presence, such as sightings and their scats," says Short.

Neither method of assessing changes in the fox population is perfect. On one hand, the number of foxes shot and recorded in the NGC might be much the same year after year, but this doesn't necessarily mean that the population is stable if the intensity of shooting has increased. It may be declining. However, the shortcomings of the BBS index are more obvious. This can be illustrated by the GWCT's practical experience when surveying breeding curlews in the New Forest. In 2020, a ground-nesting bird survey conducted by Wild New Forest recorded only six fox sightings in over 400 hours of bird survey effort involving over 1000 km of walked transects.[31] "And yet we know that gamekeepers in the New Forest are regularly killing 150 foxes a year in relatively small areas," says Short. This suggests that the BBS method of counting foxes is not a good

29. Fox - Game and Wildlife Conservation Trust (gwct.org.uk).
30. Mammal monitoring | BTO - British Trust for Ornithology.
31. A survey of ground-nesting birds in the New Forest National Park in spring 2020 to assess potential impacts of reduced recreational use, by Russell Wynn and Marcus Ward. WildNF_2020_breeding_wader_report.pdf.

way of assessing the population. The decline in sightings of foxes by BBS recorders could be a reflection of the increased wariness of the species as it has come under more pressure from gamekeepers and others.

The truth is that counting foxes accurately is remarkably difficult, as GWCT has discovered during its long-term research in Hampshire's Avon Valley, where it has been monitoring waders since the early 1990s.[32] Breeding lapwing, redshank and snipe populations have declined to such an extent here that in some areas they no longer breed at all.

GWCT scientists have a long history of tagging foxes for research purposes. In the 1990s they radio-tagged foxes on farmland about 10km away from the Avon Valley and calculated densities to be in the region of 1–2 foxes/km2. Between 2016 and 2017, they GPS-tagged foxes on a river meadow system in the upper Avon Valley. From their tagging data alone density estimates were in the region of 13 foxes/km2. However, genotyping – a genetic process akin to DNA fingerprinting – of fox scats collected in the same study area suggests that the density was much higher still. Preliminary results infer that up to 34 different adult foxes had access to this small study site.

"Frankly, we were astonished at how many foxes were living in this area," says Short. "Most of these foxes were known to be resident, but others may simply have been transients passing through. These sort of fox densities are what we are accustomed to seeing in cities, not on water meadows once important for breeding waders."

The message from the Avon Valley is that the fox population there was much higher than previously thought. In contrast, many of the people we spoke to for the Rural Wrongs project maintained that the fox population in their areas had been significantly reduced.

UNTANGLING THE TRUTH

A GWCT study, published in 2000, looked at the impact of different methods of fox control in mid-Wales, the East Midlands and West Norfolk.[33] Those involving the use of dogs accounted for 73% of foxes killed in the hilly sheep country of mid-Wales, compared to just 11% in West Norfolk, which has long been dominated by commercial shooting estates. Here, the vast majority of foxes were killed by gamekeepers, not hunts or gun packs using dogs, as in Wales. The study found that a high

---

32. The fascinating journey of a fox GPS-tracked in the Avon Valley - Game and Wildlife Conservation Trust (gwct.org.uk).
33. Heydon MJ, Reynolds JC. Demography of rural foxes (*Vulpes vulpes*) in relation to cull intensity in three contrasting regions of Britain. J Zool. 2000;251: 265–276.

cull, by whatever means, was associated with low fox density, and a low cull, as in the prime hunting country of the East Midlands, was associated with high fox density. Ignoring for a moment the method of dispatch – killed above ground by hounds, dug out using terriers, shot or snared – the fox population was higher in hunting country than in areas where game shooting and sheep rearing encouraged more rigorous methods of control.

For the *Rural Wrongs* project, we travelled to four different areas in lowland England – East Anglia, East Sussex, Surrey and Gloucestershire – to talk to people involved with hunting, shooting and farming about the current status of the fox. Everywhere we heard the same story: shooting of foxes had become more widespread and intense, mirroring the intensification of the game shooting industry and the development of highly efficient night-vision equipment. One of the conclusions of the GWCT's three-region study was that fox hunting had a restraining influence, with landowners instructing their keepers to leave some foxes for the hunt, rather than eradicate them all. In many areas, this no longer applies.

"Some places around here are now a desert as far as foxes are concerned," says Robert Bucknell, Essex farmer and the author of *Foxing with Lamp and Rifle*. "Twenty or so years ago the local hunts would always find a fox. If they were still hunting now, they wouldn't." He attributed this, in part, to the technological advances in shooting equipment. "The old method of lamping, the way we used to kill foxes, is like the Stone Age compared with what we have now." Lamping, carried out at night, involved shining a light and shooting with a rifle or shotgun any fox caught in the beam. "With modern digital night-vision equipment, you can see the red eyes of a fox half a mile away and it doesn't even know you're there," continues Bucknell. "You just squeak it in, mimicking the sound of a wounded animal, and shoot it. And if you use thermal viewers and scopes they have even less chance of escaping."

Philip Hague, huntsman with the VWH Foxhounds, whose country is in Gloucestershire and Wiltshire, is one of many huntsmen who have seen a significant decrease in fox numbers. "In the 1980s, we'd find foxes everywhere we went," he says. "In the 1990s, the numbers started declining largely because of lamping, especially on shooting estates. But the speed of decline has increased rapidly since the hunting ban in 2004." Andrew Hazeltine, huntsman with the Surrey Union, and Rob Williams, huntsman and master with the East Sussex and Romney Marsh, have all seen the fox population dwindle due to excessive shooting.
Tony Holdsworth, former huntsman with the Tiverton and later the

Duke of Beaufort's Hunt, says that as soon as he announced before a hunt, immediately after the ban, that they were going to hunt within the law everything changed. "A lot more foxes were shot as farmers and landowners knew we weren't going to kill foxes on their land. They just got others to do it instead." And they did it much more efficiently, at least in terms of numbers killed.

A local terrierman, who asked not to be named, points out that foxes are now persecuted year round. "As soon as the ban came in, it was open season on the fox," he recalls. In some areas, they have been much more hard-hit than in others. "If you go one side of a certain road near here, you won't find any foxes there now because of the shoot. Go the other side, where there is no shooting, and you can find a fox under almost every bush." Besides gamekeepers killing foxes, there are men who set their lurchers on foxes, often without landowner's permission, and there are others, not directly associated with rural occupations, who enjoy foxing at night. "There's been a serious loss of respect for the fox since the ban," says the terrierman.

The growing economic importance of shooting has meant that there has been an increase in the intensity of shooting predators like the fox over much of rural Britain. "When I left the Tiverton Foxhounds in Somerset in 2001, there were just three shoots there," says Tony Holdsworth. "There are now over 40. In the Beaufort country, there were around 10 shoots in 1985. There are now more than 65."

A well-managed shoot can not only yield a good income for the owner, but deliver important benefits for habitat and wildlife. To give just one example, measures introduced at the Duke of Norfolk's estate at Arundel, Sussex to encourage the breeding of grey partridge – such as planting hedges, protecting field margins and providing winter feed – benefited many other red-listed farmland birds besides the partridge, whose population rose from three pairs to some 300 in just 12 years.[34]

When I visited the estate in 2015, the density of corn buntings was 10 times greater than in other parts of the South Downs. Skylark numbers had tripled during a four-year period and the lapwing population had more than doubled. Indeed, lapwings on the estate produced an average 1.5 surviving chicks per pair each year, whereas chick survival was just 0.1 per pair on other parts the South Downs, even on land managed by the RSPB. The secret lay in what the late Dr Dick Potts, former director of the Game Conservancy and advisor to the Duke, described as a three-legged stool: good habitat management, effective predator control and the provision of sufficient food.

Unfortunately, there are a significant number of intensive shoots which ignore these principles. We heard this on Exmoor and in the Borders, and again in Gloucestershire. In the Beaufort country, according to Holdsworth, you would be hard-pressed to find any coverts – copses or woodlands – on shooting land which don't have pheasant pens. "In most, you won't find a fox," he says.

Lord Mancroft, who hunts with the Beaufort, illustrates the point with this story. "In the old days, in the hill country near here you couldn't see more than a few feet in the woods the undergrowth was so dense. There was thick ground cover, and any number of small birds and wild flowers. Then a shoot was set up there in the late 1980s. Now there's very little undergrowth at all, it's all been pecked out by pheasants and partridges. From a horse you see dead rats lying around – I don't know what they die from – and the ground is carpeted with the acid from accumulated bird shit, not wild flowers." The foxes have virtually gone, and so has much of the wildlife.

THE LOSS OF HUNTING'S SOFT POWER

Hugh Percy, the 10th Duke of Northumberland, was master of his own pack, the Percy, from 1940 until his death in 1988. For most of his time as Master, he hunted the hounds two days a week. It is said that if he turned up on one of his many tenanted farms and failed to find a fox, his agent would soon be on the phone to berate the farmer. As a result, his 50-odd tenants made sure there was always a fox or two on their land. It was a matter of *les paysans obliges.*

Rob Williams, master of the East Sussex and Romney Marsh and chairman of the RS Surtees Society, which was established to keep the works of the great Victorian author in print, talks about hunting's soft power. "Before the ban, there was a social contract in the countryside whereby many estates always made sure there were a few foxes for the hunt," he recalls. The vast majority of landowners recognised that hunting was about much more than controlling foxes. It was about community, culture and tradition.

"It's about the event," he says. "I routinely get text messages from hunting farmers on Romney Marsh asking me to bring hounds soon. Because it is a high point. I remember an old chap who lived right in the middle of nowhere, and he said he always loved 'to see the colours trot in', and get a nip of whisky and a free sausage roll. Modern farming can be a lonely business and a Meet is an exciting social event to brighten up the winter. Then they all jump on a quad bike and see the fields they farm unlocked by the chase."

But now, he says, hunting's soft power has faded and foxes are being hammered year round on many estates. You hear a similar story wherever you go in lowland England. "Before the ban, old keepers would always leave a few foxes for the hunt," recalls Tony Holdsworth. "But that's all changed and for many young keepers foxing is now a field sport they actively enjoy." And it is one their employers are happy to encourage.

Some landowners still support their local hunts and want to see the fox survive. One of the farmers we met in the Beaufort country – a good age now but once a regular rider with the hunt – says he has noticed a sharp decline in fox numbers since the ban. "There's been a loss of respect for the fox among many of my neighbours." This particular farmer is in an area where there has been a long-term badger cull to reduce the incidence of bovine TB, a disease transmitted from badgers to cattle and vice-versa. He won't allow the cullers onto his farm because many shoot foxes whenever they see them. This is a story we frequently heard in southern England. It adds further credence to huntsman Tony Holdsworth's paradoxical claim: "We were the fox's only friend."

MORE CRUELTY OR LESS?

When Holdsworth was huntsman with the Tiverton in Devon, he spent a good deal of time on lambing calls. Farmers who were losing lambs would ask him to come and find the guilty fox, or foxes, and kill them. "For every 10 foxes we caught and killed, I reckon nine had been injured by shot guns or snares, or they were diseased, or they were old and had lost their teeth," he recalls. These foxes, most in poor health, would have been hard pressed to catch a rabbit or a vole, which is why they went for lambs.

In the wild, there is no such thing as a good death. There are no hospices or pain-numbing opiates for sick, wounded or geriatric foxes. There is death by disease, starvation or misadventure. And there is death by human agency, which mostly involves shooting and snaring or, to use the colourful language of the League Against Cruel Sports, being ripped apart by hounds. The question is: which of these is the best way to go from a fox's point of view?

Organisations representing the shooting industry, as well as the anti-hunting League Against Cruel Sports, have always claimed that shooting causes little or no wounding. A peer-reviewed study carried out in 2003/4 by Dr Nick Fox, a biologist, internationally renowned falconer and expert on wildlife management, refuted this.[35] The study involved 199 shooters of varying skills and experience taking shots at life-size, fox-shaped paper targets under a range of different shooting regimes. These were then examined by two veterinary experts to determine whether the shots would have led to an outright kill, a serious wound, a light wound or a miss. The study suggested that shooting could potentially cause high wounding rates, with the use of shotguns – for example, when lamping at night – maiming as many as it killed.

One of the shooters to take part in this trial was Essex farmer Robert Bucknell, quoted earlier in the chapter. He believes that the move away from lamping with shotguns to using high-powered rifles with night-vision equipment has made fox shooting more efficient and more humane. "Last year, my gamekeeper shot at 51 foxes and he picked up every one. He won't squeeze the trigger unless he is sure he will kill the fox." With modern equipment, you would struggle to miss a fox unless you were very unskilled, were using a poor rest for the rifle or took a chancy shot at long range.

However, anecdotal evidence suggests that there are still plenty of people in the countryside using shotguns, often carelessly, and causing significant levels of wounding – and therefore suffering. "We now see a lot more foxes with shotgun wounds, and foxes with gangrene, than we did before the ban," says a former master of one of the Sussex hunts. Instead of leaving them to suffer, she and other hunt supporters knock them on the head with a spade or whatever comes to hand.

If you want to significantly reduce the fox population, the best time to shoot or snare them is between March and July. This is when sheep are lambing and ground-nesting birds like curlew, lapwing, golden plover and redshank are nesting. Fox control at this time of year has a significant downside from an animal welfare point of view, as gamekeepers and others will frequently shoot milky vixens. This means that their cubs will starve in their earths unless the keepers go to the trouble of finding and killing them. This is one of the reasons why conservation groups like the RSPB will not shoot foxes at this time of year. It may also explain why many nature reserves have a poor record of conserving ground-nesting birds – unlike grouse moors, where predators like foxes, feral cats and crows are ruthlessly controlled.

Many MPs voted for a hunting ban in 2004 because they were convinced

---

35. Fox, N. C., et al. "Wounding rates in shooting foxes (*Vulpes vulpes*)." Animal Welfare 14.2 (2005): 93-102.

that the field sport was cruel. They failed to take account of the alternatives, which in the case of the fox means mostly shooting and snaring. Most of the huntsmen I have talked to claim that the fox is dead within 20 seconds of being caught by the lead hound. The 2000 Report of Committee of Inquiry into Hunting with Dogs in England and Wales, the Burns Report, agreed: "in the vast majority of cases the time to insensibility and death is no more than a few seconds". Anti-hunting organisations dispute this and claim that the kill is often not instant. I imagine that in a few cases this may be true, although we are talking about a matter of minutes at the most, rather than the days and weeks of suffering caused by shotgun or rifle wounds. I should add that I have been out on a fox shoot on three occasions and on each a fox was wounded and escaped, presumably to die later of its wounds or hunger.

In his *Reminiscences of an Old West Country Clergyman*, written in the late 1800s, The Rev WH Thornton, a man who was as passionate about hunting as he was about the Eucharist, discussed at length the cruelty involved in field sports.[36] "I cannot... believe that the fox feels frightened until he begins to feel exhausted. He has escaped similar perils ever since he was a little cub, and he thinks he will escape them again. No doubt the ending is bad, but he is saved sickness, starvation, and want in old age... Besides, the beast owes his existence and long toleration to the chase. If there were no hounds there would be no foxes, and those which presently exist would perish much more miserably in gins and by poison. Shooting is undoubtedly much more cruel, because of the wounded which escape."

Of course, times have changed: gin traps and the use of poisons have been outlawed, and modern shooting equipment is far more accurate than the guns used in Victorian times. The Rev Thornton maintained that hunting was the least cruel method of dispatching foxes, but he was referring to the killing of foxes above ground by hounds, not the practice of using terriers to dig out foxes which are then shot.

Prior to the ban, approximate 40% of the foxes killed by hunts were dug out by terriermen. From an animal welfare point of view, terrier work is more problematic than the pursuit and killing of foxes above ground. Hunting with hounds is a practice as natural as a pack of wolves' pursuit of its prey, with fit, healthy foxes having every chance of escaping. Digging out foxes that have gone to ground is pest control. It can be a time-consuming affair and there is little or no chance of the fox escaping, however fit and healthy he or she is. More about this in the next chapter.

36. *Reminiscences of an Old West Country Clergyman* by WH Thornton, edited by Duff Hart-Davis, Excellent Press, Ludlow, 2010. First published 1897 & 1899.

It is true that the old dispensation, where hunting acted as a restraint on killing, has been much weakened, but a whole range of other factors determine whether the fox population is going up or down in any given area. Some of these – such as the introduction of night-vision shooting equipment and the expansion of the game shooting industry – may have led to more foxes being killed. On the other hand, the staggering number of game birds released by the shooting industry – over 50 million a year now – has created a massive new food source for a whole suite of animals, including foxes, badgers, rats, kites, crows and buzzards. Likewise, the increase in environmental stewardship schemes has led to an increase in the populations of voles and rats, much to the benefit of the fox.

In view of the significance of the fox and the important role it plays in the countryside – as predator, scavenger and object of both love and loathing – it seems astonishing that no serious research has been commissioned in recent years to establish the state of its population and the factors influencing it. This should be a priority.

An autumn sight in the lowlands that may disappear forever – huntsman Rob Williams takes the East Sussex and Romney Marsh hounds over newly cut stubble to the next draw

(Photograph: Ro Older)

A FOX AT FULL SPEED.

(CHRIS STRICKLAND)

Chapter 6
THE WELSH EXPERIENCE

In lowland England we were told that foxes had been virtually wiped out in some areas but continued to thrive in others. We heard much the same from hunt staff and farmers in South and West Wales. Some fox populations have been much reduced by shooting, while others, especially around large blocks of forestry, are prospering. Whether this is a good or bad thing depends on your point of view. However, there is widespread agreement that shooting foxes to protect livestock, game birds and ground-nesting species like curlew is very different from killing foxes for the sheer pleasure of killing.

Will Pinkney, professional huntsman with the Carmarthenshire Hunt, reckons the fox population in his area has been reduced by at least half in recent years. He doesn't object to the activities of gun packs who use dogs to flush foxes from cover in order to shoot them. These packs, registered with the Federation of Welsh Packs, have long played an important role in controlling the fox population. It is the hobby shooters, as he calls them, who are a problem.

"I really hate them, these boys from the towns and villages," he says. "They come out at night and shoot foxes and anything else they see – badgers, deer, rabbits – for the fun of killing. Then they'll post videos of the foxes they've killed on Facebook and boast about it. I saw one video of a pregnant vixen that had been shot and you could see the cubs squirming inside her belly. They think that's funny."

Simon Jones was huntsman with the Cresselly Hunt from 2003 to 2021. Before he left Pembrokeshire, he frequently received photographs sent by hobby shooters who had been on a killing spree. "There would be maybe 10 or 12 foxes hung over a fence with a gun next to them – making it obvious where they were, so I'd know what they'd done and where they'd done it. This is killing for fun and totally indiscriminate." The hobby shooters evidently saw the huntsman as a guardian of the fox, hence the pleasure in goading him. Jones estimates that the fox population has fallen by half in some areas. "But it's patchy – it varies from one area to another."

There are no gun packs operating in this part of South Pembrokeshire and most of the game shoots in the Cresselly's hunting country are relatively small. "You'll still find plenty of foxes in these places," says Hugh Harrison-Allen, master of the Cresselly, "which just goes to show that you don't have to kill all the foxes to run a good shoot." With 14 small farms on his estate, a pack of hounds, 30 cottages and a fine pub, Harrison-Allen has a good insight into the way people feel about foxes. "The problem with the Hunting Act," he says, "is that it led to a change of attitude. When the hunting ban came in, some farmers said, 'Bugger it, let's massacre the foxes', and they let anyone who wanted to shoot foxes come on their land. They wouldn't have done that before the ban."

According to Dylan Evans, master of the Tivyside Hunt, fox numbers in his country are nowhere near what they used to be. "Every Tom, Dick and Harry seems to be involved in shooting now, and we often pass four, five foxes that have been shot when we are out with the hunt," he says. The Tivyside is mostly sheep country and many farmers now allow shooters on their land. In the past, the Tivyside hounds played an important role tracking down lamb-killing foxes in the spring. "Eighty per cent of the time you'd get the right one, the one killing lambs, whereas nowadays people who go shooting foxes at lambing time might kill 8 or 9 without getting the one that's causing trouble." Unlike the hunt, shooters are taking out healthy foxes, not just the weak and sick.

The master and huntsman of a pack of beagles, formerly used for hunting hares in Carmarthenshire, tells us about a 2500-acre hill farm which kills as many foxes as possible, some 150, year after year. "It's been absolutely brilliant for brown hares," he says. "There are now lots more there than there used to be." But other areas, especially where there are large blocks of commercial forest, are still teeming with foxes. A huntsman with a pack of mink hounds in an area where the terrain makes shooting difficult says the fox population has surged in recent years, and the hare population has consequently declined. If we had spent another fortnight talking to people in different parts of Wales, I think we would have heard much the same story: foxes are being hammered in some areas; they are thriving in others.

WHY WE NEED TO KILL FOXES

While we were on our Welsh travels, Jim Barrington told me about a debate at the Game Fair in which he featured alongside Joe Hashman, a hunt saboteur as reviled by hunters as he is lauded by animal rights activists, and Robbie Marsland, Director of the League Against Cruel Sports in Scotland. Barrington explained to the audience that most of our apex predators, such as wolf, bear and lynx, had been exterminated centuries ago. As a result, carnivores of medium size – meso-predators like foxes and badgers – have no natural enemies. As the apex predator now, we humans have to make decisions about which species to control and where and when to intervene. One of the species we need to control is the fox.

Marsland responded by saying that if it was really necessary to kill a fox that was causing trouble, then it should be shot – providing you could be absolutely sure you got the right one. Hashman interrupted and said that wasn't true: there was no need to kill foxes at all as their population would simply self-regulate once it reached a certain level. In practical terms, this would mean many more foxes dying of starvation and disease. This is the logical consequence of a purist animal rights argument. It would also mean many more foxes and therefore higher levels of predation on, for example, species like curlew and lapwing. Indeed, the failure to control meso-predators like the fox and badger has had a significant, and sometimes devastating, impact on other wildlife.

Several years ago, I visited the 12,000-acre Knarsdale Estate in Northumberland. On the grouse moors and surrounding in-bye land the gamekeepers here were fighting a continuous war against generalist predators like fox, stoat and carrion crow. A four-man team of ornithologists led by a licensed bird ringer had recently carried out a survey of the estate. They estimated that during the summer, Knarsdale had at least 400 breeding pairs of curlew, 800 pairs of lapwing, 100 pairs of golden plover, 200 pairs of snipe and 50 pairs of woodcock. They also identified 22 red-listed species.[37] During my brief visit on a cold April day I saw ring ouzels, peregrine and merlin as well golden plover and curlew.

"Going there was like going to wader heaven," the lead ornithologist told me when I rang him. "I've never seen so many waders in such a small area." He added that although he and his colleagues hadn't used the standardised methodology of the British Trust for Ornithology (BTO) for counting birds, he stood by these figures. If anything, he thought they might be an underestimate.

His home patch was Dartmoor, which is topographically similar to the Northern Pennines and should, in theory, support large numbers of

---

37. In a vituperative blog attacking an article in the *Spectator* by Matt Ridley (*https://markavery. info/2016/08/14/notsotalented-viscount-ridley/*), environmental campaigner Mark Avery ridiculed these figures. The fact is that vigorous predator control means grouse moors support large populations of waders and other ground-nesting species that are generally much rarer elsewhere, even in nature reserves. If driven grouse shooting were banned many landowners would replace heather moorland with plantations of Sitka spruce, leading to a dramatic loss of biodiversity.

upland bird species. But it doesn't. Dartmoor is 20 times the size of Knarsdale, yet during recent years just one pair of curlew and five pairs of lapwing had nested there and their chicks had rarely survived. That was partly due to disturbance by grazing animals, dog walkers, mountain bikers and off-road vehicles. More importantly, there was virtually no predator control: the populations of ground-nesting birds were being suppressed by huge numbers of foxes and crows. One of the inconvenient truths about good wildlife management in the UK is that the survival of some species depends on the control of others.[38]

Which brings me to a conversation I had with Stuart Llewellyn, who I got in touch with after I returned home from our Welsh trip. By profession a heating engineer, Llewellyn's passions – as it says on his Twitter account – are fishing, shooting, conservation and river habitat restoration. I rang him because I had seen one of his posts on Twitter about the state of a local nature reserve managed by Wildlife Trusts Wales on Denbigh Moors. This is the story he told me.

He had a contract to kill foxes for a sheep farmer who lambs outdoors and he puts a lot of effort into this, not just for the farmer's sake but to reduce fox numbers near the Curlew LIFE project on the neighbouring nature reserve. The project aims to reverse the decline of these charismatic wading birds. "One night, after I had shot 4 or 5 foxes on the farm, I decided to go on the Curlew LIFE area," he recalled. He put a fox caller, imitating the distress calls of an injured prey species, on the bonnet of his vehicle. Within 10 minutes, three foxes appeared from three different directions, attracted by the noise.

"If the reserve had been controlling their numbers properly, I wouldn't have seen any," said Llewelyn. "There are signs up saying that you'll see black grouse leks and hen harriers on the reserve. No, you won't, all you'll see is foxes and crows." As he wrote in the tweet I had seen: "It is unforgivable that such a lacklustre effort is being put in to save some of our most endangered species here in Wales by [environmental] NGOs." If you do want to see black grouse in north Wales, then you need to visit Ruabon Moor, which is a keepered grouse moor, not a nature reserve.

"If you're controlling foxes for conservation purposes," explained Llewellyn, "it's important to start culling before Christmas. The success of the enterprise depends entirely on the commitment and effort of the

---

38. None of this is to deny that some gamekeepers persecute raptors. As the editor of *Shooting Times*, Patrick Galbraith, wrote in *The Critic* (Dec 22/Jan 23): "It is absolutely the case that there are moors where gamekeepers have illegally skewed the balance. Birds of prey have been killed and, in some instances, grouse have been medicated up to their beady little eyeballs in order to sustain artificially dense populations."

gun. If by March or April you go two weeks without seeing a fox, you're getting where you should be. With my curlew plots I have to be ruthless, so I am out in all weathers." It is sometimes claimed by foxhunters that hunting with dogs helps to conserve ground-nesting birds, but this is wishful thinking, especially as hunting tends to weed out the sick and injured, leaving fit and healthy foxes to go about their business. And hunts, even when operating legally before the ban, would seldom have reduced fox numbers to the level where they no longer posed a threat to ground-nesting birds.

Indeed, it doesn't require many foxes (or badgers) to have a devastating impact on ground-nesting birds. This is illustrated by the experience at Elmley, a privately-owned National Nature Reserve on the Isle of Sheppey in Kent.[39] Some 600 lapwing now breed on the grazing marshes every year, but not long ago the population was in serious trouble. A survey in the 1990s discovered that each pair of lapwing was rearing between 0.3 and 0.5 fledged chicks a year – well below the level of 0.7 needed if the population was to remain at the same level. As a result, much more effort was put into controlling predators of chicks and eggs. Foxes were shot; crows, magpies, stoats and rats were trapped; hedgehogs were caught live and transported to sites elsewhere in England.

Another survey was conducted in 2010. This compared the number of fledged chicks per pair of lapwing at Elmley, at an adjacent reserve with exactly the same habitat run by the RSPB, at another reserve on the Isle of Sheppey and at an area of grazing marsh which wasn't under conservation management. In the first year of the three-year study, the number of fledged chicks per pair at Elmley – the only place that vigorously pursued predator control – was 1.33, almost double the number required to keep the population stable. The figures for the other three sites – the RSPB reserve at Spitend, Swale National Nature Reserve and Wall End – were 0.28, 0.11 and zero respectively. Here, the lapwing was heading for extinction. These three marshes were subject to little or no predator control programme.

Llewellyn and others like him have nothing in common with the hobby shooters we heard about in South and West Wales. "We are shooting foxes with the objective of conserving wildlife and game birds or protecting livestock," he said. "They are killing for fun. For them, a night without killing is a failure. For me, it's the opposite. It means I've done my job properly." Unlike the hobby shooters, he will never shoot a milky vixen – unless it's absolutely unavoidable; for example, if the vixen

---

39. Merricks, Philip. "Comment: lapwings, farming and environmental stewardship." *British Wildlife* 22.1 (2010): 10.

threatens nesting curlews.

He was sceptical about the claim that there were more wounded foxes in the countryside since the hunting ban. If there were, he said, it was most likely that the foxes had been injured by rimfire ammunition used by lampers. But nobody in his part of North Wales goes lamping now. "I can count on the fingers of one hand the number of foxes that have made it to 100 yards after I've shot them, and I've never not picked up a fox I have hit," he said. As for the fox population, there had been no decline in his area as far as he could see. "I'm shooting the same number of foxes now as I was 10 years ago."

SUFFERING IN CONTEXT

"It's important to distinguish between suffering and cruelty," says Dr Nick Fox. "Suffering is the experience of physical or mental pain, felt by the victims. Cruelty is taking pleasure in inflicting suffering, or at least being indifferent to it. What matters as far as our discussions about field sports and other activities affecting wildlife are concerned is suffering."

We spent our last evening in Wales at Fox's Carmarthenshire farm, which is the headquarters of International Wildlife Consultants Ltd, of which he is founder and director. A wildlife biologist, falconer, farrier and livestock farmer, Fox is something of a Renaissance man. Over the past half-century, he has helped to re-establish the goshawk and red kite populations in Britain, he has introduced beavers on his farm, he was the lead author of the fox-shooting study referred to in the last chapter, and he has directed numerous research programmes, many focusing on the breeding and conservation of birds of prey as far afield as New Zealand, China and Kazakhstan. He is master of the Northumberland Crow Falconers, the oldest mounted falconry group in the UK, and he hunts with the Pembrokeshire Foxhounds.

Fox has spent a good deal of time thinking and writing about animal welfare. His 1996 *An investigation on behalf of the Hawk Board into the nature and extent of suffering caused by current methods of pest control and field sports* is one of the few attempts to set hunting with hounds within the context of other activities involving the killing of wild animals.[40]

To discuss this and other matters, he had gathered together a group of people involved in hunting for dinner at his farmhouse. These included

---

40. Fox, Nick, and Helen Macdonald. "An investigation on behalf of the Hawk Board into the nature and extent of suffering caused by current methods of pest control and field sports." International Wildlife Consultants Ltd, 1996.

his partner Helen Nakielny, an expert on sight hounds and currently undertaking a doctorate on the use of robotic prey for falconry, sisters Ruth Rees and Margaret Johns, joint masters of the Pembrokeshire Foxhounds, and Greg Baker, joint master and huntsman with the Llandeilo Farmers Hunt. Early discussions focused on the state of the fox population. The joint masters of the Pembrokeshire told a familiar story: in some areas the fox was much reduced, in other areas it was doing well. Greg Baker had much the same to say about hobby hunters as the other huntsmen we had met: he deplored the lack of respect for the fox and the way the shooters boasted about their feats on social media.

Much of what Fox wrote in his investigation for the Hawk Board is relevant today, even though hunting with dogs has been banned. He analysed a range of activities – from the use of gazehounds, scent hounds, terriers, ferrets and falcons to shooting, live trapping, snaring, poisoning and cat predation – in terms of categories, including natural selectivity (whereby weak and infirm individuals are more likely to be caught than healthy ones); legal selectivity (where only legally unprotected target species are captured); pre-capture pursuit interval (the length of time from the start of the prey taking evasive action to its capture or escape); and catch-to-kill interval (the length of time between the initial physical contact between predator, or weapon, and prey and the latter's death).

Only two methods score well on all points: gazehounds like lurchers or greyhounds pursuing hares and rabbits, and raptors, such as falcons killing carrion crows. Scent hounds follow close behind, scoring well in most categories. The use of terriers and ferrets to bolt foxes and rabbits underground is not without problems as it is difficult to supervise and intervene, for example if a terrier attacks a fox. Domestic cats and traps both score badly and government-approved poisons are responsible for suffering on a massive scale, causing prolonged severe pain and distress to at least 20 million small mammals each year.

The scale of killing matters too. Prior to the hunting ban, registered and unregistered packs of hounds in Britain killed approximately 25,000 foxes, hares, deer and mink a year. In contrast, Fox calculated that in the mid-1990s, some 9 million domestic cats in Britain killed at least 88 million birds and 164 million small mammals. Furthermore, cats kill in such a slow way, amounting to a form of torture, that they have frequently been selected as a model animal for studies of predatory and aggressive behaviour.

A study published in April 2022 estimated that cats kill 160 to 270 million animals a year, of which about a quarter are birds.[41] This pretty much confirms Fox's 1996 figures. "The impact of domestic cats is huge – not just in terms of the numbers of wild birds and mammals they kill, but the suffering they cause," said Fox. Neither politicians nor organisations like the RSPB, who one would expect to take an interest in the massacre of British birdlife, dare to upset the many millions of cat owners by highlighting the issue or calling for significant curbs on a cat's right to roam. This is astonishing – and cowardly – when you consider that domestic cats killed approximately 82% of wild animals killed by the activities investigated by Fox in the mid-1990s. Shooting accounted for around 6% and hunting with dogs 0.006%.

"Many of the anti-hunting organisations are funded by cat-keepers who maintain that because they do not enjoy watching their cats mauling birds, they are therefore eliminated from the charge of cruelty," wrote Fox in his study. "The lack of human enjoyment is not relevant to the suffering animal, whereas the negligence of the owner, in preventing it, is."

In 2017, Baily's Hunting Directory published a study carried out by Dr Helen Brook, a chemist (and owner of Baily's with her husband Peter) who used applied scientific principles to evaluate the suffering caused by a similar list of activities to the one used by Fox. She came to much the same conclusions: hunting with hounds scored highest among the animal control methods she investigated for reasons already discussed here. Prior to the ban, packs traditionally focused on one or two types of quarry; they tended to target weak, old and injured animals, rather than the fit and healthy; the numbers caught per day were generally very low; the fox either got away unharmed or it was killed; and hunting ceased during the breeding season.

Many consider terrier work, or digging out as it is sometimes called, to be one of the more worrying aspects of hunting. One person who was candid about the subject was the 10th Duke of Beaufort, who wrote about it in his book *Fox-hunting*, published in 1980. Terrier work, he argued, was necessary. However, if it wasn't undertaken by the hunts under controlled conditions, "it would be undertaken by others under a totally opposite set of conditions: one of extreme cruelty and brutality. Better by far to be dug out and either shot cleanly in the head or killed with a sharp blow, than to be smoked or dug out and then clobbered to death with a shovel, or torn to pieces by three or four bloodthirsty

---

41. Pirie, Tara J., Rebecca L. Thomas, and Mark DE Fellowes. "Pet cats (Felis catus) from urban boundaries use different habitats, have larger home ranges and kill more prey than cats from the suburbs." *Landscape and Urban Planning* 220 (2022): 104338.

terriers."[42]

It is worth pointing out here that hunting with dogs, as defined in the legislation, covers a range of activities involving different breeds. Foxhounds, staghounds, otter hounds, and beagles and bassets were bred to pursue fox, hare, otter and hare respectively, all of which they pursue, or pursued, above ground.[43] They might also kill the odd rabbit or cat, but that's pretty much the extent of their predatory activities. Lurchers, which are a cross between a greyhound or other sight hound and a different type of dog, such as a sheep dog, were bred to hunt hares, rabbits and small deer. That's pretty much the extent of their predatory activities. Neither hounds nor lurchers can be used underground or as fighting dogs.

Terrier work is a different matter and it is important to stress that there are two very different categories of terriermen (terrier work is mostly a male occupation). On one hand, there are the terriermen whose activities are regulated by the hunts and who follow a code of practice laid down by the National Working Terriers Federation (NWTF).[44] They use "soft" terriers which stand and bark, rather than attack the fox. Radio collars on the terriers help to locate the fox in its earth. The fox is eventually flushed into a net and killed humanely with a bullet to the head. This is the acceptable face of terrier work.

Unfortunately, there is another group of "hard men with hard dogs" who revel in setting their animals on foxes and badgers and encourage them to fight underground. You only have to look at some of the photographs of terriers posted on social media sites, with their torn ears and scarred faces, to see these are fighting dogs bred to attack. People who indulge in this form of animal killing are cruel and sadistic. Not surprisingly, hunt terriermen and terriermen abiding by the NWTF code of practice take exception to being lumped together with these people.

Under the 2004 Hunting Act, a single dog can be used to flush out wild mammals solely for the purpose of preventing or reducing damage to game birds or wild birds which are being preserved in order to be shot. Leaving aside the ludicrousness of this injunction – you can't use a terrier to flush out foxes which are killing lambs or rare ground-nesting birds like curlews, lapwing and redshank – the law does genuflect in the direction

---

42. This was the view of the Burns Report: "Although there is no firm scientific evidence, we are satisfied that the activity of digging out and shooting a fox involves a serious compromise of its welfare, bearing in mind the often protracted nature of the process and the fact that the fox is prevented from escaping.

43. After otters were afforded full legal protection, otter hounds were used to hunt mink, an exotic riverine species that was having a devastating impact on native wildlife like the water vole.

44. Home (terrierwork.com).

of reducing suffering. Under the Act, terriermen must do everything they can to reduce the amount of time taken to flush out the fox. Care must be taken to avoid injury to the terrier. All hunt terriermen must be licensed and in possession of a firearm for which they hold a valid certificate.

As far as I know, no scientific research has been done in this country on what happens between dog and fox underground, but it seems inevitable that there must be a degree of suffering, mental if not physical, as far as the fox is concerned. It is not in a position to flee, as foxes above ground flee from hounds; indeed, flight is part of their evolutionary history. It is effectively trapped until the terrierman digs down and dispatches it, or it is flushed into a net and shot.

I have frequently been told by hunts that many farmers insist they can only come on their land if foxes which go to ground are flushed out and killed. I am sure this is true, especially in hill country and areas of rough pasture where farmers want to protect their lambs. In which case, I can see the 10th Duke of Beaufort's point of view: better to have a licensed terrierman under the control of a hunting organisation dig out and kill the fox, rather than a bunch of blokes using more aggressive breeds of terrier and looking for a bit of "sport" after closing time at the pub.

When assessing whether a particular method of killing animals should be tolerated or not, there are two key questions. First, we should ask: if we ban such-and-such a way of killing animals – hunting with hounds, for example, or using terriers to dig out foxes – will it be replaced with methods which cause greater suffering? And second: is the suffering experienced by an individual animal – such as a stag being chased to a standstill – justified if the activity involved, in this case hunting with hounds, delivers long-term benefits to the population as a whole, for example in terms of the health and vigour of the herd?

At the kennels of the Pembrokeshire and Carmarthenshire Minkhounds. During a scheme to eradicate American mink in the Outer Hebrides, mink hounds found the invasive predators in areas where trapping had failed.

(Charlie Pye-Smith)

According to a post mortem report, this vixen had survived severe rifle shot wounds – shattered jaw, eye missing, tongue severed – before it was killed by the Llanbrynmaer Foxhounds in March 2004.

Chapter 7
ANIMAL RIGHTS, RURAL WRONGS

It seems extraordinary that almost two decades after the 2004 Hunting Act came into force the issue of hunting with dogs is unresolved. Nobody is happy: neither the hunters who feel that their activities have been severely curtailed, nor the animal rights activists who campaigned for a ban. Tony Blair's "masterly British compromise" has been nothing of the sort. It has made matters worse for the hunted species, not better. It has led to an increase in conflict in the countryside, not peace. And the Hunting Act was so poorly drafted it has been hard to enforce.

As far as I can tell, people who hunt – and I am referring here to the staff and followers of registered packs – have taken three different approaches to the ban: the ostrich, the kamikaze and the rational.

A pro-hunting Tory MP whom I met at a friend's funeral several years ago had this to say when I asked whether his party would repeal the Act: "Best not to rock the boat and just leave things as they are – after all, most hunts are still going out." This head-in-the-sand approach is doomed: the Labour Party, which at the time of going to print is odds on to win the next general election, has pledged to tighten up the Hunting Act. This may well mean that trail hunting – following a pre-laid scent, rather than a wild animal – with a pack of hounds will be illegal. If that happens, there will be no point in keeping the hounds: most will get a bullet in the back of the head.

The second approach – the kamikaze – has been adopted by those who are convinced that it is only a matter of time before the scenario described above takes place. They think they might as well go out in a blaze of glory, hunting as though the Act did not exist, and enjoy themselves before the sun sets on their fieldsport. This, I suspect, is precisely what Mr John Jorrocks, RS Surtees's cockney huntsman and one of the great creations of Victorian literature, would do were he alive today. I have no idea how many of the 170 or so registered packs of foxhounds in England and Wales were still hunting foxes, rather than following a trail, when Jim Barrington and I undertook this research. It might have been a dozen; it might have been many more.

The third approach assumes, optimistically, that we live in a rational world where logic will eventually triumph over sentimentality and prejudice; that if it can be shown that the Hunting Act has failed to improve animal welfare, then MPs will agree to repeal or reform it. This seems to be the approach taken by the British Hound Sports Association (BHSA), which was established in mid-2022 as the governing body for all the hound sports associations in England, Wales and Scotland. It believes that hunts must demonstrate that they are abiding by the law and that they are not using trail hunting as camouflage for the real thing. Only then will it be in a position to start campaigning for new legislation.

The BHSA is playing a long game and it is too early to judge how effective it will be, but at least it has acted with commendable speed when presented with evidence that hunts have broken the law. In February 2023, footage gathered from a mobile phone taken by the police showed a fox being extracted from an earth and thrown to a pack of hounds by the Avon Vale Hunt.[45] Those present, including hunters on horseback, were clearly taking pleasure in doing something that was both cruel and illegal. The BHSA's disciplinary panel immediately suspended the hunt and later expelled the masters, huntsman and kennel huntsman from the BHSA.[46] It later announced a permanent ban on the hunt. Without BHSA membership it will be almost impossible for the hunt to operate.

Time is certainly not on the hunters' side. The current Conservative government won't touch the subject, not least because there is now a significant body of Tory MPs who would like to see the sort of changes to the Hunting Act proposed by the Labour Party in its 2019 Animal Welfare Manifesto. This called for harsher penalties, including custodial sentences for those breaking the law; for the introduction of a new recklessness clause to prevent trail hunts being used as cover for illegal hunting; and for the removal of the exemption for "research and observation", which would probably mean an end to stag hunting.

In January 2023, the Scottish Parliament passed the Hunting with Dogs (Scotland) Act. This ignores one of the key recommendations in Lord Bonomy's report on the Protection of Wild Mammals (Scotland) Act 2002. The Bonomy report, commissioned by the Scottish National Party (SNP), stated that flushing foxes from cover in order to shoot them was more efficient with a full pack of hounds than with just two dogs. The new law stipulates that a maximum of two dogs can be used. If a farmer or landowner wants a hunt to use more they will need to apply for a licence. This legislation will almost certainly make matters worse for the

---

45. 'Sickening' video obtained by ITV News 'shows illegal fox-hunt in progress' | ITV News.
46. BHSA, Avon Valley Hunt Disciplinary Hearing, 9 February 2023.

welfare of the fox, not better. It could also criminalise rough shooters who use dogs to bolt rabbits and other game.

The new law prohibits trail hunting too. This means that a group of consenting men, women and children are banned from following, on horseback or on foot, a pack of hounds which chase an animal-based scent. This is defined as a scent which is either derived from a wild mammal, for example fox urine, or which mimics the scent of a wild mammal, even if it is made from artificial ingredients. "However," says clause 99 of the Act magnanimously, "a trail of beef sausages would not fall within the definition because this would not mimic, replicate or resemble the scent of a wild mammal."

Reading through the discussions at the report stage of the bill it is clear that for many Scottish politicians their animus was against mounted packs, which are associated with hunting as a sport, rather than foot packs operating a pest control service. During one of the committee hearings, a representative for the foot and gun packs claimed that his members did not enjoy what they did. I think this is nonsense. Of course they enjoy it. But he realised that this claim would chime with politicians' Calvinistic disapproval of people having fun on horseback. From a hunted fox's point of view, it makes not a whit of difference whether the people chasing it are enjoying themselves or not.

Shortly before we visited South Wales, reports on social media claimed the Labour-controlled Welsh government and Natural Resources Wales (NRW) had decided to phase out all field sports in the principality. This turned out to be untrue, but there was a general feeling among those we interviewed that both the devolved government and NRW have become increasingly hostile to hunting and shooting.

In 2021 the Board of NRW voted to approve changes to its licencing system that mean gamekeepers and others can no longer control magpies, jackdaws and jays for conservation purposes. NRW has also limited the time window when carrion crows can be controlled for conservation purposes. According to research commissioned by NRW, the curlew could be on the verge of extinction in Wales in the next decade without serious interventions. Yet restrictions on controlling its aerial predators will simply hasten its demise, rather than the opposite. Many other ground-nesting birds will also suffer from the new restrictions.

The Welsh government has recently voted to ban snares, including humane cable restraints used for foxes – the only form of snare to comply with the Agreement on International Humane Trapping Standards.

Like the restrictions on conservation licences and general licences, this is bad news for ground-nesting birds predated by foxes. This means the government agency charged with wildlife conservation in Wales has introduced measures, presumably for ideological reasons, that will almost certainly hasten the decline of some species.

NRW is one of the largest landowners in Wales. In November 2021, it banned trail hunting on its property after Mark Hankinson, then director of the Masters of Foxhounds Association (MFHA), was found guilty of encouraging hunts, during a Zoom meeting, to use trail hunting as a smokescreen for illegal fox hunting. His conviction was later quashed on appeal. The fact that NRW and many other public bodies reacted to the original findings of the court case by banning trail hunting on their land was understandable. None, as far as I know, have rescinded the ban following Hankinson's successful appeal.

Our last field trip was to Northern Ireland, the only part of the United Kingdom where hunting has not been banned or severely restricted. Although the Northern Ireland Assembly was suspended, we still managed to talk to politicians as well as people involved in the hunting world. The previous year, when the Assembly was still sitting, a bill to ban hunting, proposed by Alliance Party member John Blair, was voted down.[47] Had it become law, the Hunting of Wild Mammals Bill would have prohibited all forms of hunting with dogs, including the use of terriers to flush foxes from underground, and outlawed trail hunting as well. Although the bill failed in 2021, it could well be revived after a new Assembly is convened.

Those who wished to maintain the status quo in Northern Ireland were hoping that *Rural Wrongs*, once published, could be used to convince wavering members of the Assembly that banning hunting would do nothing to improve wild animal welfare. The stakes are high. The hunting debate in Northern Ireland is not just about animal welfare and class; it is about community cohesion. "When you're out on the hunting field in Northern Ireland, politics and religion are left behind," said one master of foxhounds. "Hunting is one of the things that unites us."

THE BALANCE SHEET

So what exactly did we discover on our travels?

Staghounds in the West Country can only use two dogs under the 2004 Act. This has made it much harder to find and dispatch deer which have

---

47. Hunting bill: NI politicians reject hunting with dogs ban - BBC News, 6 December 2021.

been hit by vehicles or wounded by shooters than it used to be with a full pack of hounds. As the hunts can no longer go out with a full pack they are failing to disperse herds across the landscape. As a result, red deer are now congregating in larger numbers and becoming more vulnerable to infectious diseases like bovine TB. More red deer are now being shot, both legally and illegally, than in the past and an increase in poaching has led to more deer being wounded.

When it comes to the fox population it is hard to disaggregate the impact of the Hunting Act from the impact caused by the intensification of game shooting and the availability of high-tech night-vision shooting equipment. In many parts of the country foxing has become a field sport in its own right, practiced not just by gamekeepers but by individuals who take pleasure in killing foxes and boasting about it on social media. The scale of killing is undoubtedly greater in some areas than it used to be, leading to a significant decline in fox numbers. Yet in other areas foxes are doing well. There is no doubt that restrictions on hunting have led to a loss of respect for the fox among many landowners and farmers.

One of the reasons why hunting organisations have struggled to justify their activities is because the rationale for hunting varies from one part of the country to another. In hill country, hunts and gun packs have always played an important role in reducing the fox population before and during the lambing season. Indeed, the use of hounds is the best way of identifying and removing lamb-killing foxes. Calling in shooters, on the other hand, often means that foxes which are not causing problems are being killed unnecessarily, or wounded, especially when shotguns are used rather than rifles.

In the lowlands, fox hunting is not so much about pest control as wildlife management. If anything, it has acted as a restraining influence, encouraging shooting estates to leave a few foxes rather than wipe them out. Indeed, the beauty of fox hunting in the lowlands is its inefficiency. Huge amounts of effort are expended on killing relatively few animals. Before the ban many hunts would kill just 30 or 40 foxes in a season, amounting to not much more than a single fox killed for each day's hunting. If you Google "shooting foxes" on YouTube you will see plenty of footage of shooters killing 20 or more in a single night. Many of the videos are made for entertainment with jaunty, blokes-in-a-pub commentary and mood music.

Foxes which are chased above ground either get away unharmed or die swiftly in the mouth of the hounds. The healthier and fitter they are, the more likely they are to escape. The issue of terrier work, which involves digging out foxes that have gone to ground, is more controversial. This does not involve instant death and it can take considerable time from the introduction of the terrier to the earth to the shooting of the fox. Even if terriers don't attack the fox underground, it is reasonable to assume the latter suffer a level of stress.

As far as the brown hare is concerned, the Hunting Act, which banned both competitive hare coursing under National Coursing Club rules and hare hunting with hounds, was indirectly responsible for a dramatic increase in illegal hare coursing. This generally involves gangs of men who have no compunction about attacking landowners, farmers and gamekeepers who try to prevent them trespassing. Illegal coursing is frequently associated with farm thefts and damage to property. During the days after the hunting ban came into force in 2005, over 3000 hares were shot on two estates in East Anglia, not to make jugged hare but to ensure that the estates would not be targeted by illegal coursers. We heard frequent stories of farmers shooting all the hares on their land to keep the illegal coursers away. This is a fine example of the unintended consequences of bad law.

But then this was to be expected. The Minister responsible for introducing legislation to ban hunting, Alun Michael, cherry-picked the evidence gathered in 2002 at the Portcullis House hearings into hunting with dogs, which he chaired, and he did the same with the report of the Inquiry into Hunting with Dogs in England and Wales. Lord Burns, who chaired the inquiry, had this to say in the House of Lords: "I struggle enormously to see how [the Hunting Act] passes Alun Michael's test that the legislation should be soundly based and should stand the test of time."[48] The inquiry, as Lord Burns pointed out, did not have sufficient evidence to reach a clear conclusion as to whether hunting with dogs involved significantly worse welfare for the fox.

In a letter to Simon Hart, then chief executive of the Countryside Alliance, Prof Sir John Marsh, a member of the inquiry, repeated the comments made in the House of Lords by Lord Burns, before adding: "The report was careful not to reach conclusions about cruelty. There was insufficient evidence upon which to do so. Describing as we did the final moments of the hunt as 'seriously compromising the welfare of the hunted animal' should not be taken to suggest that hunting was measurably worse than other legal methods, or that abolition would improve the plight of wild animals in the countryside."

The Hunting Act was largely influenced by animal rights, rather than

---

48. Lords Hansard text for 12 Oct 2004 (241012-09) (parliament.uk).

animal welfare, considerations. Advocates of animal rights believe that every sentient creature should be allowed to live without human interference or exploitation. The Hunting Act was designed to prevent an activity – in this case hunting with dogs – from causing suffering to individual animals. It was not concerned with the welfare of the species. But any meaningful and workable legislation needs to take account of both.

I believe that animals do not and cannot have rights. "Humans have rights because we are rational beings, who exist by negotiation and by the reciprocal recognition of duties," wrote the philosopher (and fox hunter) Roger Scruton. "A creature that cannot recognise the rights of others cannot claim rights for itself. Only if animals had duties, therefore, would they also have rights. But it would then be wrong to capture them, kill them, eat them, to keep them as pets, to train them to stand on their hind legs or to make use of them in any way."[49]

It should go without saying that the way animals are killed matters: it should be as humane as possible. That means we need to establish which methods are acceptable and which are not. You could certainly argue that it is better for a fox to be swiftly killed above ground by hounds than to die slowly and painfully from shotgun wounds. We also need to think about the welfare of the species, which means there might have to be trade-offs. Take, for example stag hunting. I quite understand that many consider it cruel that stags are chased to the point of exhaustion. However, there is no doubt that stag hunting on Exmoor has helped to establish the fittest and healthiest red deer herd in the UK. Recent research suggests that deer which are no longer moved around and dispersed by the hunt are now carrying higher levels of infectious disease. Dying slowly from bovine TB is almost certainly a greater cause of suffering than being hunted and shot over the course of an afternoon.

One of the great tub thumpers on the subject of fox hunting is the *Guardian* columnist George Monbiot, the closest thing the radical greens have to a high priest. In a much quoted article published during the hunting debate in 2004, Monbiot argued that we needed a ban because it would help to create a more classless society, not because it would do much for animal welfare. In his view, fox hunting ranked about number 155 as an animal welfare issue. Indeed, in one of his polemics Monbiot recognises that hunters have a vested interest in maintaining the species they hunt. In *Feral*, a sort of Bible for rewilders, he looks forward to the day when wolves will be reintroduced to Britain. Hunting, he argues, could be the

---

49. *Against the tide: the best of Roger Scruton's columns, commentaries and criticism*, edited by Mark Dooley, Bloomsbury, 2022.

wolves' salvation, creating a powerful lobby for their protection, "just as anglers have become the staunchest defenders of fish stocks."[50]

Our research suggests that hunters – whether of fox, deer or hare – are, or were, great defenders of the species they hunt, although Monbiot didn't recognise this, so obsessed was he with the class war. This strange paradox, the love of a creature and passion for hunting, is brilliantly described in Nancy Mitford's *The Pursuit of Love*: "The Radletts loved animals, they loved foxes, they risked dreadful beatings in order to unstop their earths and rejoiced over Reynard the Fox, in summer they got up at four to go and see the cubs playing in the pale-green light of the woods; nevertheless, more than anything in the world, they loved hunting. It was in their blood and bones... and nothing could eradicate it, though we knew it for a kind of original sin."

The killing of large animals almost certainly influenced the mating behaviour, language, art and spiritual beliefs of early humans. Hunting, in other words, helped to make us what we are today. "Even though he lived by hunting, primitive man worshipped animals," wrote the scientist and environmentalist René Dubos, whose book *So Human an Animal* won the Pulitzer Prize for non-fiction.[51] "In modern man also, the desire to hunt is paradoxically compatible with love of wildlife."

THE BIGGER PICTURE

In 1985, on the margin of the negotiations which led to the Anglo-Irish Agreement, a conversation took place between Seán Donlon and Robert Armstrong (later Lord Armstrong of Ilminster). Donlon was involved in negotiations on behalf of the Irish government; Armstrong, Margaret Thatcher's Cabinet Secretary, was doing the same for the UK. "I was moaning about the fact that so much political debate in Ireland was narrowly focused on abortion and divorce," Donlon told me when he heard I was writing about the Hunting Act. "Robert responded by saying there were similar problems on the British side, but the issues were different: 'We are preoccupied with Sunday opening and fox hunting,' he said."

This conversation took place almost 40 years ago, reflecting decades of obsessional interest in – and opposition to – hunting with dogs, particularly among Labour MPs. It was an obsession that never went away and it helps to explain why an absurd amount of time was spent

50. *Feral: Searching for enchantment on the frontiers of rewilding* by George Monbiot, Allen Lane, 2013.
51. *So Human an Animal: How We Are Shaped by Surroundings and Events* by René Dubos, Scribner, 1968.

debating and discussing the hunting issue in Parliament in the early years of this century, why sentimentality frequently trumped science, why many MPs were not remotely interested in the facts, why some of the discussions would have disgraced a moderately intelligent class of 10-year-olds. When it comes to an obsession, logic is little more than a bee sting on a pig's backside.

I am not going to rehearse what I have already written about this in *Rural Rites*. Suffice it to quote Peter Oborne, then political editor of the *Spectator*, in his introduction. The book, he suggested, was an essential read for anyone who wanted to understand how Britain was governed at the start of the 21st century: "Viewed from this perspective Pye-Smith's book is terrifying. It demonstrates that we are ruled by emotion rather than logic, by ignorance rather than knowledge, by bigotry rather than understanding."

Plus ça change, plus c'est la même débâcle.

While we were researching *Rural Wrongs*, I kept an eye on the campaign to ban the importation of hunting trophies, such as the skins, heads, horns, tusks and other derivatives of animals like lion, elephant, giraffe and eland. In March 2023, The Hunting Trophies (Import Prohibition) Bill, tabled by Conservative MP Henry Smith, received its third reading and was passed unopposed. Many of the MPs' contributions to the debate, and the campaigning material on which they based their pronouncements, were breathtaking in their mendacity and ignorance.

I have taken more than a passing interest in the subject as I spent several weeks in Southern Africa during the late 1990s talking to local communities and conservationists about the benefits of well-regulated trophy hunting. In the deeply impoverished part of Zimbabwe where I spent most of my time, profits from trophy hunting had enabled villagers to build classrooms and health clinics, hire teachers and nurses and establish income-generating projects like grinding mills. Instead of seeing wild animals like elephants and lions as a threat to their survival and killing them, as they did in the days before they could benefit from trophy hunting, they were now protecting them.

Most of the MPs who spoke in favour of the ban got their information on the subject from the Campaign to Ban Trophy Hunting, whose director provides secretariat services for the all-party parliamentary group which supports the ban. A group of scientists, including Amy Dickman, director of the Wildlife Conservation Research Unit (WildCRU) at Oxford University, and Adam Hart, Professor of Science Communication at the University of Gloucestershire, both of whom have long experience working with wildlife and communities in Africa, analysed 118 statements made by MPs during one of the parliamentary debates. They found that 85 were either false or misleading. These included all nine statements made by Conservative MP Sir Roger Gale and 29 out of the 37 statements made by the bill's proposer, Henry Smith.[52]

In its desire to blacken the concept of the sustainable use of wildlife, the Campaign to Ban Trophy Hunting was greatly bolstered by the support of celebrities, the vast majority of whom have little or no experience of life in rural Africa – except, I imagine, as guests of high-end safari lodges. They specialise in emotive hyperbole: "appalled and disgusted" (TV presenter Lorraine Kelly), "the sport of rich psychopaths" (actor Ricky Gervais), "the lowest of the low... utterly grim and cruel" (actress Joanna Lumley), "a sport for morons, cowards and bullies" (explorer Sir Ranulph Fiennes), "senseless cruelty" (comedian Bill Oddie). Many other well-known figures, none of whom, as far I could gather, had any expertise in the subject – including Frank Bruno, Kate Moss, Gary Lineker, Boy George and Delia Smith – put their names to a letter in *The Times* grandly claiming that "it would be a crushing blow to democracy" if the Hunting Trophies (Import Prohibition) Bill failed to become law.

"Every Western democracy is being debased by a type of celebrity-politico class which imagines that shouting dumb stuff out loud gives heroic purpose to their lives," suggested the political commentator Douglas Murray when reflecting on football pundit Lineker's likening of the government's language on immigration to that of the Nazis in the 1930s.[53] If further proof of Murray's contention were needed, several MPs were as intemperate in their views as the celebrities quoted above, with Sir Roger Gale excelling himself during the trophy hunting debate. "What we're talking about is gratification of the most revolting kind that I would compare with paedophilia," he said.

Similarly tasteless language has been routinely used by those opposed to field sports like fox hunting. "Hunting... belongs to that class of always impermissible acts along with rape, child abuse and torture," wrote the Rev Prof Andrew Lindzey, a member of the Faculty of Theology in the University of Oxford. To those who have been raped, abused and tortured, this statement by an Anglican priest must sound utterly preposterous.

---

52. In areas outside protected areas where rural livelihoods and domestic livestock are threatened by wildlife, and where villagers receive none of the benefits which accrue from trophy hunting, lions and other animals are much more likely to be killed by poisons, snares and crude weapons. These frequently cause much greater suffering than a trophy hunter's bullet.
53. The overuse and abuse of "fascism" by Douglas Murray. *Spectator*, 18 March 2023.

BBC wildlife presenter Chris Packham recently had this to say on Twitter about fox hunters: "They shoot their hounds, they whip their hounds, they punch their horses. They kill people's pets, damage their property, break the law and rip our diminishing wildlife to pieces for fun." This stereotype was based on a few instances of bad behaviour, but it does not provide a complete or fair picture of hunting. Yes, a woman had been filmed punching her horse just before Packham wrote this tweet. Yes, hunts occasionally kill people's pets. Yes, hunts do put down their hounds by shooting them. And then, as we have seen, there have been occasions when hunt staff have behaved appallingly, as in the case of the Avon Vale Hunt, which was described in the last chapter.

However, Packham's claim that hunting is ripping our diminishing wildlife to pieces is absurd. If the fox population is declining, it is because large numbers are being shot and snared, not least because the restraining influence of the hunt has declined since the Hunting Act came into force. There are all sorts of reasons why our wildlife is "diminishing" – intensive agriculture, monoculture forestry, chemical pollution, urbanisation – but hunting with dogs is not one of them.

Anti-hunting campaigns rely heavily on whipping up public opposition. Apparently, 86% of Britons and 92% of Tory voters support the ban on importing hunting trophies. But this is a very complex subject and you can be absolutely sure that the vast majority of those canvassed by polling companies had never heard the conservation and livelihood arguments in favour of trophy hunting. They certainly won't have seen the letter to *Science* magazine entitled "Conservationists should support trophy hunting" and signed by over 100 scientists and researchers, or the open letter from over 50 community leaders in Africa urging celebrities in the UK to stop "undermining the human rights of impoverished people and jeopardising wildlife conservation in the region." This was a polite way of saying: kindly check your white privilege.[54] Well, our politicians didn't listen. The Hunting Trophies (Import Prohibition) Bill was passed by the House of Commons in March 2023 with the backing of the Conservative government. Like the 2004 Hunting Act, this was a triumph of ignorance and populism over science and good sense. At the time of going to press, the Bill was being scrutinised in the House of Lords and a series of pro-conservation, pro-community amendments meant that it was by no means certain to become law in its present form.

The vast majority of those asked by pollsters whether they are in favour of retaining the ban on hunting in this country will have little or no idea about the complexities of wildlife management, or the unintended

54. See, for example: Conservationists Should Support Trophy Hunting (perc.org), 6 September 2019.

consequences of the ban highlighted by this report. And why should they? I can think of dozens of important subjects about which I have no knowledge at all. So if there's a message here to MPs it is this: do your research properly, suppress your prejudices, look at every side of the argument, ignore opinion polls and treat with suspicion any individual or organisation who is frothing at the mouth with anger and resentment.

EPILOGUE

On Boxing Day 2022, my wife Sandie and I came across a great stream of cars and walkers going into the park at Petworth House in Sussex, so we followed with our dogs. They were gathering for a meet of the Chiddingfold, Leconfield & Cowdray Hunt. About 50 riders milled around outside the kennels under a watery sun, chatting among themselves and to friends and strangers among the crowd of some 300 people. They were of every age and class, most dressed in the apparel of country dwellers, many taking an interest in the hounds which wagged their tails in anticipation of a day's trail hunting.

There was nothing to suggest, in the demeanour of the crowd and the conversations overheard, that events such as these, a feature of Boxing Days stretching back more than a century, might soon be a thing of the past. They almost certainly will be if a future Labour government acts on a pronouncement made that day by shadow environment secretary, Jim McMahon, in the pages of the *Guardian*. If elected, he said, Labour would put an end to trail hunting, as this is widely used as a smokescreen for illegal fox hunting.

Were this to happen, it would mean that the innocent – the registered packs who are trail hunting within the law – would be punished for crimes they had not committed. It would be like banning the serving of strong liquor in public houses on the grounds that it encourages alcoholism; or closing down public lavatories as they are sometimes used for cottaging. It would be an act of deep illiberalism. The presumption of innocence till proved guilty, a right which can be traced back to Magna Carta, would be sacrificed in pursuit of what former Labour home secretary Jack Straw described as a "nonsense issue".

When asked for his response, Lord Herbert, the chairman of the Countryside Alliance, told *The Spectator*: "Labour's position is utterly illogical and the large number of prosecutions under the Hunting Act only shows that the legislation is perfectly effective."[55] This view, as he later explained in an article for *The House*, was a call for the Labour Party to drop its obsession with the issue and remove it from the political agenda.[56] However, it suggested to some that the Countryside Alliance

---

55. Labour's fallacious fox hunting battle | *The Spectator*, 26 December 2022.
56. Is it time to ban trail and drag hunting? Lord Herbert says No (politicshome.com).

was taking a cautious approach by suggesting the legislation was effective.[57]

A more robust response to the threat of restrictive legislation has come from a new rural pressure group, Hunting Kind.[58] Established in 2021 by Ed Swales, a former army officer and security expert who lives and hunts in northern England and southern Scotland, Hunting Kind champions natural forms of hunting "that don't involve a hook in the mouth or a bullet in the head," as Swales puts it. He has teamed up with This is Hunting UK, and between them they have some 100,000 Facebook followers. What distinguishes Hunting Kind from other hunting groups is that it appeals to a broad swathe of people associated with working class pursuits such as terrier work, ferreting and the use of lurchers, as well as to traditional foxhunters. If the Labour government does decide to introduce a complete ban on hunting, some of Hunting Kind's followers won't roll over meekly.

Nobody immersed in the issue thinks the Hunting Act should be maintained in its present form. The hunters believe the Act has seriously curtailed or undermined their activities. The antis – including the well-funded campaigners of the League Against Cruel Sports and the paramilitary-minded saboteurs – also believe the Act has failed, although for different reasons. The 2004 Hunting Act is not, and never was, fit for purpose. Indeed, this has been confirmed by the person who was given the task of drafting the legislation, senior parliamentary draughtsman and barrister Daniel Greenberg. Speaking to the Surtees Society in 2020, Greenberg suggested that the "clearest proof that this was never a measure aimed at improving animal welfare is that nothing in the construction of the legislation tends towards its effective enforceability as a matter of animal welfare."[59] The legislation, he believes, was driven more by moral outrage than animal welfare.[60]

As we have seen, there is much talk among opponents of hunting about "tightening up" or "strengthening" the Hunting Act. This invariably means getting rid of exemptions – such as those which allow stag hunts to use two hounds rather than a full pack – and possibly outlawing trail hunting. If the latter happens, there would be no point in hunts continuing to operate and many would put their hounds down. Without the support of subscribers they wouldn't be able to afford staff, kennels or hounds.

---

57. The vast majority of the 430 or so convictions under the Hunting Act since 2010 have been for poaching, not for activities carried out by employees of registered hunts.
58. Hunting Kind - The opportunity to make the voice of the 'Rural Voter' heard.
59. See, for example: R.S. Surtees Society | A Learned Society dedicated to the works of RS Surtees | "First They Came For the Hunts – Lessons from an Insider's View of the Hunting Act for the Role of Tolerance in the Rule of Law" By Daniel Greenberg.
60. Hunting Act driven by moral outrage, not animal welfare, says man who wrote law (telegraph. co.uk), 26 September 2022.

I have spoken to some hunters who say that they will continue hunting even if hunting is completely banned. Packs of hounds could be split up and "trencher fed", with members of the hunt taking home a couple apiece and meeting to hunt. In more remote parts of the country, I doubt if the police would have the time or inclination to do anything about such breaches in the law. As for the proposal, made by some politicians and endorsed in its manifesto by the Green Party, that the use of dogs underground to locate or flush out foxes should be banned, all I can say is: good luck with that! They obviously haven't canvassed the views of terriermen or gamekeepers, or considered the difficulty of policing these activities. A ban on terrier work would almost certainly push the practice, metaphorically as well as literally, underground. Terrier work would no longer be subject to the codes of practice laid down by the National Working Terriers Federation (NWTF), with grave implications for the welfare of the fox (and badger).

In Scotland, the devolved government has already shown that it is not interested in evidence: it simply despises the practice of hunting, particularly where it involves the presence of people on horseback. It seems perfectly possible that a Labour government in Westminster, acting either alone or in coalition, would pursue a similar policy of restricting hunting to such an extent that it becomes no more than a form of pest control, despite the fact that some of the worst abuses of animals are done in the name of pest control.

So for the sake of our wildlife – and especially the fox, the red deer and the brown hare – the 2004 Hunting Act should be replaced. But with what? On this matter I defer to Jim Barrington, who has spent a good deal of his life contemplating the various pieces of legislation which affect wildlife, initially as an employee and then director of the League Against Cruel Sports and later as a key player in the All Party Parliamentary Middle Way Group, which published *Rural Rites*, and as adviser on welfare matters to the Countryside Alliance.

In the early years of the century, during Labour's second term in power, Barrington was closely involved with the Labour peer Lord Donoughue, who championed two bills which sought to improve wild animal welfare. Both received overwhelming support from all sides in the House of Lords and were welcomed by countryside agencies such as the National Farmers' Union (NFU), the Country Land and Business Association (CLA) and the Countryside Alliance. The Wild Mammals (Protection) (Amendment) Bill, which was introduced in the House of Lords in 2003 and in the House of Commons in 2004, would have made it a criminal offence to cause unnecessary suffering to any wild mammal. Had it passed, accusations of cruelty could have been tested in a court of law, just as they are in the case of domestic animals, on the basis of evidence presented. However, the bill was talked out in the House of Commons. Nothing was going to induce the MPs who were obsessed with banning hunting to vote for legislation which would have made the 2004 Hunting Act irrelevant.

There is, fortunately, a legal precedent for what Lord Donoughue and his supporters hoped to achieve. This is the Welfare of Animals Act (Northern Ireland) 1972, which granted protection not only to domestic and captive animals but to all animals, including hunted species such as the fox, hare and deer. Under the 1972 law, hunting, coursing and fishing were exempt, unless they involved activities which caused "unnecessary suffering". In other words, any individual or organisation who believed hunting, or any aspect of it, was responsible for causing unnecessary suffering was free to test the evidence in court. Unfortunately, the 1972 Act was superseded by the Welfare of Animals Act (Northern Ireland) 2011. This removed the clause about unnecessary suffering and thereby the route to prosecution.

There is no reason why something similar to the 1972 Act should not be introduced in Westminster for England and Wales, and in Holyrood for Scotland. This would take the vexatious subject of hunting off the political agenda and allow the courts to make decisions on the basis of the evidence they received.

The idea that the 2004 Hunting Act should be replaced with legislation similar to the 1972 Act produced a priceless response from the then chief executive of the League Against Cruel Sports, Douglas Batchelor. "The problem with that suggestion is that someone would actually have to be cruel to an animal before they could be charged with any offence," he said. Well, yes: surely that is the whole point of good animal welfare legislation.

Most of the MPs who voted for the 2004 Hunting Act clearly had a poor understanding of both wildlife management and wild animal welfare. The Act has been a dismal failure and it should be replaced with legislation that benefits both the quarry species and rural communities. As Prof John Webster wrote in *Animal Welfare – Limping Towards Eden*: "It requires very little knowledge to care passionately about animals. It requires a great deal of understanding to care properly for them."[61] It is time for Parliament to make amends.

---

61. Webster, John. *Animal Welfare: limping towards Eden: A practical approach to redressing the problem of our dominion over the animals.* John Wiley & Sons, 2008.

MILES COOPER IS ONE OF SEVERAL FORMER EMPLOYEES OF THE LEAGUE AGAINST CRUEL SPORTS WHO DECIDED THAT A HUNTING BAN WOULD DO MORE HARM THAN GOOD. WHIPPING IN FOR THE HUNSLEY BEACON BEAGLES NEAR HULL.

(PHILIP REESE)

RURAL WRONGS DONORS

Viscount Astor, Michael Baines, the Beaufort Hunt, Richard Boggis-Rolfe, C Z Corrie, Mrs Antoinette Galbraith, Nicholas Hornby, O H Inskip, Robert Jones-Davies, Sam Kershaw, Stephen Lambert, T Lewis, Dora Loewenstein, Tom Lyle, Mrs AJR MacPherson, Charles Mann, Christopher McEwan, Jess Leigh Pemberton, Simon Richards, Andrew Riddick, Christopher Rose, Maxwell Rumney The RS Surtees Society, Richard Schuster, Susan Simmons, Robin Smith-Ryland, Snowdon Farms, Luke Tomlinson, Mark Tomlinson, Richard Tyacke, Rosie Vestey, Robin Vestey, James Murray Wells, Lord Willoughby de Broke.

PEOPLE WE INTERVIEWED FOR RURAL WRONGS AND OTHERS WHO HELPED US

Tim Allen, Alan Anderson, Jo Aldridge, Arron Atmore, Greg Barker, Sam Bell, Claire Bellamy, George Bowyer, Dr Jen Brewin, Dr Helen Brook, Peter Brook, Robert Bucknell, Andy Byatt, Ed Coles, Dr Keith Collard, Prof. Jaimie Dick, Duane Downing, Dylan Evans, Guy Everard, Ian Farquhar, Pammie-Jane Farquhar, Rowley Fenwick, Dr Nick Fox, Geoff Garrod, Richard Griffiths, Di Grissell, Gardie Grissell, Charles Harding, Hugh Harrison-Allen, Andrew Hazeltine, DJ Heston, Matthew Higgs, Robbie Keith Hodge, Baroness Hoey, Tony Holdsworth, Lulu Hutley, Margaret Johns, Simon Jones, George Logan, Dr Declan Looney, Stuart Llewelyn, Baroness Mallalieu, Lord Mancroft, Bill Montgomery, Liz Mort, Helen Nakielny, Richard Negus, Matthew Paul, Sir Mark Prescott, Will Pinkney, Ruth Rees, Countess Susie Goess-Saurau, Sir Johnny Scott, Lady Sophie Scruton, Dr Mike Short, Philip Sykes, Chris Strickland, Ed Swales, Hugh Thomas, John White, Jeremy Whitehorn, Rob Williams M.F.H, Tony Wright, Tom Yandle.

THE DESIGN AND PRODUCTION TEAM

Anya Buchan, Angus Friell, Izzy Hayes, Eleanor Crane, Harriet Lewis & Alex Lee. Sincere thanks, also, to the celebrated sporting artist and foxhunter Daniel Crane for the cover, and to Katie Baines for the proofreading.

Index

A

All Party Parliamentary Middle Way Group, 18, 85
Allen, Tim, 30, 31, 34
Atmore, Arron, 36, 39–40
Avon Vale Hunt, 72, 81
Armstrong, Lord Robert, 78

B

Baker, Greg, 65
Barrington, Jim, 8, 9, 17, 60, 85
Batchelor, Douglas, 86
Bellamy, Claire, 30, 34
Blair, Tony, 16, 17, 71
Bonomy, Lord: review of Scottish hunting legislation, 33–34
Brook, Dr Helen: study of suffering caused by different methods of pest control and field sports, 66
Brown hare: unintended consequences of bad law, 37–44; history of hunting and coursing, 38–39
British Hound Sports Association (BHSA), 72
Bryant, John, 13
BTO Breeding Bird Survey, 48
Bucknell, Robert: on illegal hare coursing, 42–44; on shooting foxes, 50
Burns Report (Committee of Inquiry into Hunting with Dogs in England and Wales), 55; Lord Burns' response to the 2004 Hunting Act, 76

C

Carmarthenshire Hunt, 59
Cash, political corruption and the 2004 Hunting Act, 14–16
Celebrities: ignorance of, 80
Chiddingfold, Leconfield & Cowdray Hunt, 83
Coles, Ed, 43–44

Collard, Dr Keith, 23
College Valley and North Northumberland Hunt, 31
Countryside Alliance, 17, 83
Cresselly Hunt, 59–60

D

Dartmoor: foxes killing lambs, 25; consequences of lack of predator control for ground-nesting birds, 61
Death in the wild: no such thing as a good death, 53
Dickman, Prof Amy, 79
Digging out foxes with terriers: percentage of foxes dug out by hunts, 27; welfare aspects of, 55, 66–68
Donoughue, Lord Bernard, 15
Downing, Duane, 40
Dubos, René, *So Human an Animal*, 78
Duke of Beaufort's Hunt, 50–52
Duke of Buccleuch's Hunt, 30

E

East Sussex and Romney Marsh Foxhounds, 50
Elmley National Nature Reserve: importance of predator control, 63
Evans, Dylan, 60

F

Fox, Dr Nick: wounding rates when shooting foxes, 54; on suffering caused by pest control and field sports, 64
Fox population in the UK, 47–49
Foxing as a field sport, 24, 59, 75
Fielding, Henry, *Tom Jones*, 15

G

Galbraith, Patrick: on persecution of raptors by gamekeepers, 62

Gale, Sir Roger, 80

Game and Wildlife Conservation Trust (GWCT): on brown hare population, 39; on fox population dynamics, 48-50

Gamekeepers: pressures on, 31; fight against illegal coursing, 42-44

Garrod, Geoff, 43

Golding, Baroness Llin, 15

Greenburg, Daniel: on the failure of the 2004 Hunting Act, 84

H

Harding, Charles, 23

Hare coursing in Ireland, 41

Harris, Prof Stephen, 38

Hart, Prof Adam, 79

Harrison-Allen, Hugh, 60

Hashman, Joe, 60-61

Hague, Philip, 50

Hazeltine, Andrew, 50

Herbert, Lord Nick, 83

Hoey, Baroness Kate, 16

Holdsworth, Tony, 50-51, 53

Higgs, Matthew, 38

Hunting Act 2004: badly drafted, 13; impact on red deer, 21-24; impact on brown hare, 37-44; impact on fox, 24-27, 47-56, 59-68, 71-86

Hunting with Dogs (Scotland) Act 2023, 29

Hunting Trophies (import Prohibition) Bill, 79-82

Hunting of Wild Mammals Bill (Northern Ireland Assembly): failure to become law, 74

Hunting Kind, 84

I

Illegal hare coursing, 37, 42-44

International Fund for Animal Welfare (IFAW), 11

J

Johns, Margaret, 65

Jones, Simon, 59

K

Knarsdale Estate, Northumberland: birdlife on grouse moors, 61-62

L

Labour Party, 2019 Animal Welfare Manifesto, 72

Lauderdale Foxhounds, 28, 30-31

League Against Cruel Sports, 11, 15, 17, 38, 53, 61, 86

Llewellyn, Stuart, 62-63

M

Mallalieu, Baroness Ann, 24-25

Mancroft, Lord Benjamin, 52

Marsland, Robbie, 61

McMahon, Jim, 83

Michael, Alun: role in Portcullis House hearings, 38-39; cherry picking evidence, 76

Mitchell, Austin, 16

Mitford, Nancy, *The Pursuit of Love*, 78

Monbiot, George, 15, 17, 77-78

Murray, Douglas: on "dumb stuff" from the celebrity-politico class, 80

N

National Gamebag Census, 48

National Trust: bovine TB in red deer on its Exmoor estate, 23

National Working Terrier Federation (NWTF), 34, 67, 84

National Resources Wales: antipathy to field sports, 73-74

Negus, Richard, 42

O

Opinion polls: why we shouldn't trust them, 80

P

Packham, Chris: opposition to hunting with dogs, 81
Pembrokeshire Foxhounds, 64–65
Pinkney, Will, 59
Police, Crime, Sentencing and Courts Bill, 44
Political Animal Lobby, 16
Potts, Dr Dick, 51
Predator control: importance for ground-nesting birds, 61–63
Prescott, John, 15
Prescott, Sir Mark, 37, 39, 44
Protection of Wild Mammals (Scotland) Act 2002: impact on the fox, 29–35

R

Red deer: their story on Exmoor, 21–27; incidence of bovine TB, 22–23, 75; impact of legislation on casualty deer, 21–22
Rees, Ruth, 64
Ridley, Jane, Fox-hunting, 14–15
Ridley, Matt: attacked by Mark Avery for claims made in the Spectator about grouse moor biodiversity, fn61
Royal Society for the Protection of Animals (RSPCA), 11

S

Scott, Sir Johnny, 31
Scottish Parliament: ignores recommendations of the Bonomy Report, 72
Scruton, Sir Roger, 7, 16, 77
Shooting: impact of intensive game shoots on Exmoor, 24–26; impact of intensive shoots in the Scottish borders, 31; virtues of well managed game shoots, 42–44; example of sustainable shooting estate in Sussex, 51
Short, Dr Mike, 47–49
Skinner, Dennis, 14, 18
Smith, Henry, 79–80

Straw, Jack, 16, 83
Swales, Ed, 31, 84

T

Thomas, Hugh, 24
Thomas, Kelvin, 25
Tivyside Hunt, 60

V

VWH Foxhounds, 50

W

Waterloo Cup, 38–39
Watts, Martin, 22
Webster, Prof John, 86
Welfare of Animals Act (Northern Ireland) 1972, 86
West Country staghounds, 21–27
Whitby, David: problems caused by intensive game shoots fn25
Widdecombe, Ann, 16
Williams, Rob, 8, 50, 52–53

Y

Yandle, Tom, 22, 26